Life under Nyerere

Godfrey Mwakikagile

Copyright (c) 2006 Godfrey Mwakikagile
All rights reserved.

Life Under Nyerere

Second Edition

ISBN-10: 0-9802587-2-3
ISBN-13: 978-0-9802587-2-1

No part of this book may be reproduced in any form for commercial purposes without written permission from the publisher.

New Africa Press
Dar es Salaam, Tanzania
Pretoria, South Africa.

American spelling is used in this book in order to maintain the integrity of the original text which was first published in the United States.

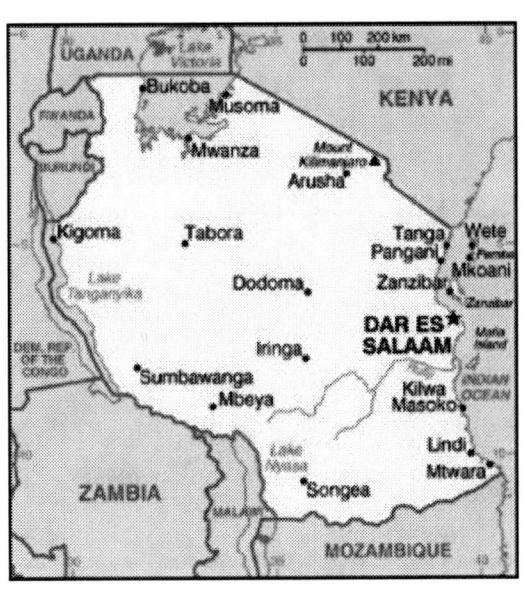

New Africa Press

Our books focus on the African world. They are intended for members of the general public and the academic community.

We cover a wide of range of subjects, reflected by the diversity of our titles, with primary emphasis on trade books. Academic works published by New Africa Press are also intended for the general public. Few titles, if any, are published exclusively for members of the academic community.

All our works are non-fiction addressing contemporary issues, history, politics, economics, international affairs relating to Africa, and many other subjects. People of African descent in the diaspora are an integral part of the African world and the focus of some of our works.

Because of the wide range of subjects we cover, some of our titles may not seem to be relevant to Africa and the African diaspora.. But many of our readers will find them to be useful if for no other reason than that their experience is human experience and the diversity reflected by our works derives its legitimacy from our identity as an integral part of humanity.

Introduction

MANY of those who were born in Tanganyika during British colonial rule are in a much better position, than those who weren't, to assess the full impact and influence of President Julius Nyerere on the country because they knew what type of leader he was since he began to campaign for independence in the early fifties, and whether or not he changed through the years.

I am one of them but not quite. I was born in colonial Tanganyika. But I was only a child when Nyerere started to campaign for independence travelling across the country to mobilize support for the nationalist struggle against British colonial rule. I nonetheless am in a position to make a fair assessment of what type of leader he was because I grew up under his leadership.

When he started his nationalist campaign in the early fifties after returning to Tanganyika from Britain in 1952, I was less than five years old. I was born on 4 October 1949 in the town of Kigoma, a port on Lake Tanganyika, in the western part of the country bordering the former Belgian Congo.

In fact, I was almost exactly 4 years and 9 months old when Nyerere formally launched the Tanganyika African National Union (TANU) on 7 July 1954. He was 32.

Seven years later, he led the country to independence when TANU won massive support across the country in one of the biggest political and electoral victories in colonial history.

Much of this narrative and analysis is written from a personal perspective. But the subjects I have addressed are national and international in scope in terms of Nyerere's leadership.

He was no ordinary man hence larger than life in terms of influence on a global scale, yet humble as a peasant in terms of his commitment to the well-being of the masses. He was their saint, and humble servant, and without whom he would not have become as a leader of international stature.

As a news reporter in Tanzania, I got the chance to know about Nyerere as a leader in a way I would never have had I gone into another field or simply stayed in my home village in Rungwe District in the misty blue mountains of the Southern Highlands of Tanzania in a region that borders Malawi, which was known as Nyasaland during British colonial rule. My home region also borders Zambia, once known as Northern Rhodesia when it was under British colonial rule.

Therefore I looked at Nyerere from a vantage point many people didn't have when he led our country and during a period when he was one of the most influential African leaders on the entire continent and indeed in the history of post-colonial Africa. He will be remembered for generations.

But I also remember him in another respect. President Nyerere was the editor-in-chief of our newspaper, the *Daily News*. Yet he did not play any executive role at the newspaper. However, his position as editor-in-chief was of highly symbolic significance since he was the embodiment of the aspirations of the masses. And our newspaper served as an organ, and as a national institution, articulating their needs and grievances. It was government-owned.

Nyerere's close ties to the newspaper were also reflected in his appointment of our editors, Sammy Mdee and Ben Mkapa, as his press secretaries at different times. It was also he who appointed them as editors.

Mkapa also served as Tanzania's ambassador to Nigeria and the United States, and as Tanzania's high commissioner (ambassador) to Canada under President Nyerere. He also became Tanzania's minister of foreign affairs under Nyerere, and eventually president of Tanzania himself from 1995 to 2005.

Nyerere left a legacy which continues to inspire millions of people in Tanzania and elsewhere especially in other parts of Africa. But it is also a legacy that has drawn mixed reactions from many other people, depending on how they saw him as a leader and what kind of policies he pursued.

I have done my best to explain some of those policies and portray Nyerere the way he was: a simple yet tough leader, an intellectual yet a humble politician, deeply committed to the well-being of his people in spite of the mistakes he made during his tenure which lasted almost a quarter of a century as president of Tanzania.

I can't and don't speak for anybody else. What I have written here is the way I saw it and from personal experience as someone who was born in Tanganyika, and grew up in Tanganyika, later in Tanzania.

I am sure there are those who differ with me just as there are those who agree with me including some of Nyerere's most ardent critics who, in spite of their criticism of Nyerere and his policies, still concede that although he made mistakes, he did his best for his people. As he himself said in an interview with the *Black World*, an African-American journal, in the early seventies when he was asked what he would like to be remember for after he died, he hoped people would say: "He did his best."

Mwalimu Julius Nyerere

Life Under Nyerere

THE DEATH of Julius Nyerere in October 1999 marked the end of an era in more than one way.

He was one of the pioneers in the struggle to end colonial rule after the end of World War II. He was also one of the first African leaders who led their countries to independence in the late fifties and in the sixties as one of the last surviving leaders who spearheaded the struggle for African independence; among them, Kwame Nkrumah, Jomo Kenyatta, Nnamdi Azikiwe, Sekou Toure, Modibo Keita, Patrice Lumumba and others. And he outlived most of them.

The only surviving former African presidents who led their countries to independence in the sixties and who outlived Nyerere were Leopold Sedar Senghor, a Francophile, who died in France in December 2001 at the age of 95; Ahmed Ben Bella of Algeria, Dr. Kenneth Kaunda of Zambia, and Dr. Milton Obote of Uganda who were also his ideological compatriots like Dr. Nkrumah, Sekou Toure, Modibo Keita, and Lumumba. Dr. Obote died in October 2005. He was 80 years old.

It was the era of "Big Men," the founding fathers, and the life of Julius Nyerere as a political leader of international stature epitomized the best among them, despite a number of failures during their tenure.

They will be remembered as the leaders who not only led their countries to independence but who also maintained national unity, especially in the early years after the end of colonial rule, laying the foundation for the nations we have across the continent today. They will also be remembered as the leaders who - besides Azikiwe and a few others - introduced the one-party system to fight tribalism and consolidate nationhood, and socialism to achieve economic development.

Nyerere will be remembered for both, probably more than any other African leader. His one-party state was probably the most successful in transcending tribalism and maintaining national unity. Tribalism never became a prominent feature of national life in Tanzania under Nyerere, unlike in other African countries wracked by war and other conflicts. And besides Nkrumah, he was also the most articulate exponent and theoretician of one-party rule.

A firm believer in socialism until his last days, he was also one of the strongest proponents of socialist policies for decades. And he lived and died as a socialist probably more than any other African leader. Even after his socialist policies failed to fuel and sustain Tanzania's economic growth, he remained a firm believer in socialism, and responded to his critics in rhetorical terms: "They keep saying you've failed. But what is wrong with urging people to pull together? Did Christianity fail because the world isn't all Christian?"[1]

It is not my purpose in this small book to examine the successes and failures of Nyerere's socialist policies but to look at how life was under Nyerere in one of the poorest and most ethnically diverse countries in Africa and, indeed, in the entire world.

These are my reflections on Tanzania, the land of my birth (it was then called Tanganyika and still a British colony), and on the life and death of Julius Nyerere, a leader my fellow countrymen and I came to know through the years as a patron saint of the masses and as one of the world's most influential leaders in the twentieth century.

His socialist policies were mostly a failure in many areas in terms of economic development, but not his ideals of equality and social justice. My life in Tanzania, like those of millions of other Tanzanians, was shaped and guided by those ideals. It is these ideals which sustained Tanzania and earned it a reputation as one of the most stable and peaceful countries in Africa, and one of the most united; a rare feat on this turbulent continent.

It was Nyerere's biggest achievement, as he himself said. And it was, even more so than the unification of Tanganyika and Zanzibar in 1964, although this also was a feat of singular significance on a divided continent.

Tanzania stands out as the only country in Africa formed as a union of two independent states. No other union has been consummated on the entire continent, setting Nyerere apart. It was he who engineered the union of Tanganyika and Zanzibar. And it was he who played the biggest role in maintaining stability of the union, and even in sustaining the union itself because of his sense of fairness and extraordinary ability in consensus building as a basis for national unity.

Although the union was indeed a big achievement, there was no question that Nyerere had other goals in that area. His biggest failure, he said, was that he did not succeed in convincing his fellow leaders in neighboring countries to form an East African federation.

But in fairness, it must be stated that it was the other East African leaders who failed to live up to their Pan-African commitment to form the federation.

Kenyatta and Obote agreed with Nyerere in June 1963 to form the East African Federation before the end of the year, but never did. The other two leaders were not as enthusiastic as Nyerere was. Kenyatta was the least enthusiastic. Obote was ideologically close to Nyerere and in his commitment to a political union of the three East African countries and, in fact, went with Nyerere to see Kenyatta and asked him if he was ready to unite. They also told him that he should be the president of the new macro-nation once the three countries united. But Kenyatta refused, as Nyerere said in an interview with the *New Internationalist* in December 1998 we cited earlier.

So, Obote would probably have united Uganda with the other two countries. But internal opposition to his rule, especially from the Buganda kingdom, precluded any possibility of fulfilling his Pan-African commitment to form the East African Federation.

Not long before he died, Obote was interviewed by Ugandan journalist Andrew Mwenda in Lusaka, Zambia, where the former Ugandan president was living in exile and had a lot to say on the failure of the East African federation. The interview was published in *The Monitor*, Kampala, Uganda, 10 April 2005, under the headline, "I Did Not Sabotage East African Federation," and Obote had this to say:

Trouble at home

Immediately after independence, we faced three major challenges: the East African federation, the organisation of the army, and the lost counties of Buyaga and Bugangaizi.

Regarding the East African federation, there have been claims from people like Museveni that I am the one who frustrated it because I wanted to be a big fish in a small pond.

The East African federation could not have been sabotaged by me. We were talking about two federations at the same time, Buganda federation within Uganda, and the East African federation.

There were problems in Kenya and Uganda which frustrated the drive towards the federation.

I do not remember the factors in Kenya. However, in Uganda, the UPC had come into government in an alliance with KY (Kabaka Yeeka) which was rabidly opposed to the East African federation.

Remember that the first time the British proposed an East African federation, there was a stand off with Mengo and the Kabaka was deported.

I find Museveni's reasoning myopic because he tends to personalise obstacles to decision making in Uganda under my administration to me personally.

As prime minister of a political party in a coalition government, I could not make decisions without bringing different interests into agreement. In fact even within the UPC itself, there was no consensus about the East African federation. For example, Adoko Nekyon, Felix Onama and Cuthbert Obwangor were opposed to the idea but I now forget on what grounds.

The second challenge was the army. Immediately after independence in 1964, the army mutinied. We had to call in British troops to cool it down.

Secondly, within a few years of independence, Grace Ibingira with Edward Muteesa began working closely with Brigadier Shaban Opolot, the army commander, to overthrow the government.

Ibingira had his own brother, Major Katabarwa in the army. Ibingira accuses me, in his books, of refusing to promote people like Major Karugaba because they were Catholics. But I promoted many officers like Brig. Okoya who were Catholics. It was Ibingira in the UPC government of 1962 who had ideas about the army.

Ibingira had started in London to pick up boys from Ankole and send them to military schools including his own brother Maj. Katabarwa. Ibingira picked up about five Ankole boys to go to military colleges.

In 1964, I supported Muteesa to become president. Muteesa knew very well that the constitution of 1962 mandated the government to hold a referendum in the lost counties for people to decide whether they wanted to remain under Buganda administration, return to Bunyoro or become an independent district.

So Muteesa wanted Buganda to retain the counties. He began to frequent the counties and settle Baganda ex-service men there with the hope of increasing the numbers of Baganda in order to create an artificial advantage.

To ensure fairness, government declared that only those who were on the voter register would participate in the referendum. In fact Muteesa one time went to one of the counties and shot people, Banyoro, dead.

Although some unscrupulous authors have accused me of promising both Muteesa and the king of Bunyoro to help them win, in a game of double dealing, that is entirely untrue.

I published all my positions, even in the UPC manifesto of the 1962 elections on the issue of the referendum. Muteesa was not a fool. Neither was Omukama a fool to see a referendum and they say Obote said "I will do this for you".

The referendum was held as per the constitution towards the end of the second year into independence and people voted by overwhelming majority to go back to Bunyoro.

I understand the difficulty such a referendum presented to Sir Edward. Although he was president of Uganda, he was also Kabaka of Buganda.

Under the constitution, he was supposed to sign the results of the referendum in order to bring them into legal effect. His dual role as president of Uganda and Kabaka of Buganda made this more difficult and he refused to sign. I do not blame him at all.

The constitution also said in the event the president fails to ascent to a bill, the prime minister can. So I signed the results because I knew that was the best way to help Muteesa out of a difficult situation.

How could a Kabaka of Uganda sign away part of his kingdom to go to another kingdom?

Some people have written saying this was the beginning of the break-up of the UPC-KY alliance. The UPC-KY alliance did not break-up. It ended in a marriage because by 1965, 16 out of 21 KY members of parliament had crossed to UPC. Therefore by the time the dissolution was officially announced, there was little left of KY.

Muteesa and Ibingira deliberately encouraged KY members in parliament to cross to UPC in order to increase the number of UPC parliamentarians who would support a plot by Muteesa and Ibingira to get rid of me. So it was not done out of good faith.

I want to comment on the 1964 UPC delegates' conference which has been a subject of much writing and much misrepresentation.

I have been accused of siding with Ibingira to remove John Kakonge from the office of secretary-general (of UPC). I was sick. I don't know if Dr. Gesa is still alive but he will tell you that I did not attend the conference. I opened the conference and I went to bed. William Nadiope who was vice president of the party in collusion with Ibingira decided to have delegations which they financed.

Nadiope took the whole of Busoga, thousands of people, to Gulu. Kakonge did not know that this group had been financed by the CIA.

Kakonge's group was accused of being communist with me in it, but Kakonge did not know.

They even gave him a CIA girl, Peace Corp volunteer to date, so that they could spy on him. When it came to the conference, Nadiope and Ibingira had filled it with their supporters and they used this numerical strength to defeat Kakonge. That is how Ibingira used CIA money to become secretary-general of the UPC.

If you read Ibingira's writings, he admits that he was plotting to remove me also from being party president so that Nadiope could take over the leadership of UPC.

Formation of OAU

In the meantime, we had other foreign affairs issues to deal with other than the East African federation. This was the height of the cold war and the world was divided between east and west. I took a strong Pan-African position in favour of a continental union.

In May 1963, I arrived in Addis Ababa where the first conference of leaders of newly independent states was going to take place.

Africa had been divided between two groups: the Monrovia group composed of conservatives, and the Casablanca group composed of the progressive radical.

The Monrovia group was opposed to Nkrumah's proposal for an immediate creation of a union government for the whole of Africa.

On the first day I arrived, my friend Kwesi Ama, a Ghanaian, came to me and said Kwame Nkrumah, the president of Ghana, wanted to have lunch with me and that I should 'expect a bomb shell'.

I had met Kwesi Ama in London. He was my friend and was Nkrumah's ambassador to London. Nkrumah was the leader of African progressive opinion. We all admired him immensely.

I personally admired Nkrumah immensely. He was an illustrious leader. He shaped African liberation and gave Africa a voice in world affairs. He supported liberation struggles all over Africa.

So meeting him was a great honour and opportunity. People like Patrice Lumumba, Julius Nyerere, Kenneth Kaunda, all progressive African leaders looked to Nkrumah.

When we sat down to lunch, Nkrumah told me there was no conference. "You should go back home." He said the Monrovia group had already sabotaged the conference. I told him that we should not go back home. We should put our case to the conference on the need for African unity.

And I told him that as far as I could see, there was possible success if only we could reorganise what we wanted the conference to do. Nkrumah said we wanted All-African Union Government.

I told him that given the polarisation, we could not achieve that. Although we could present our case for immediate African political union, we had to be careful because we could not get the majority needed to see it through.

So we had to argue our case as a bargaining tool to get the conference to form an organisation that would work towards the creation of a continental government.

I also told Nkrumah that while a continental union was a great idea, we could not wish it. We had to put in place an organisation to work towards it.

During the conference, Nkrumah made a great speech on the need for a union government for Africa.

He called for a constitution for an African continent government, a common market, an African currency, an African monetary zone, an African central bank and an inter continental communication system.

I stood up in the conference and called for the creation of a strong Pan-African executive and an African parliament to which all African governments must be prepared to surrender their sovereignty.

This position was supported by Modibo Keita, president of Mali; Sekou Toure, president of Guinea; and the president of Egypt, Gamer Abdel Nasser. All these were my friends.

My call for immediate unity was tactics. We used the Nkrumah stand to bring others opposed to African co-operation to agree that a compromise meant building an organisation to promote the ideals of unity.

Later in the conference, I suggested that since African unity cannot be achieved overnight, let us put in place an organisation to work towards the realisation of that goal.

This was a compromise position between 'unity now' and the extreme position by people like President Tsiranana of Malagasy Republic (now Madagascar), Balewa and others against African co-operation.

Then Ahmed Ben Bella of Algeria took to the floor with a moving call for African liberation. He pledged 10,000 Algerian volunteers to free African nations still under colonial oppression and white minority rule. "A Charter will be of no value to us," he said, "and speeches will be used against us if there is not first created a blood bank for those fighting for independence."

I stood up and offered Uganda as a training ground for African troops to be used to liberate African countries from colonial rule and white minority rule.

Then Sekou Toure suggested that we fix a date after which "if colonialism were not ended, African states would expel the colonial powers."

Leopold Sedar Senghor of Senegal and Nyerere stood up and made strong recommendations on building capacity to liberate the whole of Africa.

Finally we agreed to the formation of the Organisation of African Unity (OAU) whose mandate it was to end colonial rule and work towards unity.

Marriage to Miria

At the end of the conference, Nkrumah was impressed by my contribution and he cancelled his flight back to Ghana and instead came with me to Kampala where he planted a tree.

That same year I married Miria and we spent our honeymoon in Ghana with Nkrumah.

In 1965, I together with Nkrumah and Nyerere took a strong stand against

Ian Smith's Unilateral Declaration of Independence in Southern Rhodesia now Zimbabwe.

Although failure to form the East African Federation was one of Nyerere's biggest disappointments in the Pan-African sphere and in foreign policy, he also had one major achievement in these two areas as the most prominent and relentless supporter, among all African leaders, of the liberation movements in southern Africa. And he lived up to his commitment.

Tanzania under his leadership became the headquarters of all the African liberation movements and provided material, diplomatic, and moral support to the freedom fighters through the years until the end of white minority rule. But without strong domestic support, Nyerere's efforts to help free southern Africa and pursuit of his foreign policy initiatives would not have been successful. It was Tanzania's stability and mass support for Nyerere as a national leader, which made the realization of these goals possible. And it is to this domestic arena that we now turn, in my reflections on Tanzania and on the life and death of Julius Nyerere.

My life as an African has a lot in common with the lives of my fellow Africans across the continent. We all live in countries affected by one form of strife or another, differing only in degree. And we all, at least most of us, belong to one ethnic group or another. I am a Nyakyusa, one of the few ethnic groups or "tribes" in Tanzania - including the Sukuma, the largest, with more than 7 million, the Nyamwezi, the Chaga, the Hehe, the Haya - with more than one million people in a country of 126 different tribes.

Yet I am a Tanzanian first and foremost, transcending my tribal identity. Still, the tribe is an enduring entity and an integral part of Africa. You cannot define Africa without it, or even begin to understand Africa without comprehending its nature and the central role in plays in life across the spectrum in most African countries.

Call it an ethnic group, a term sometimes more acceptable than tribe because of the latter's derogatory connotation applicable mostly in the African context, while deemed inappropriate and irrelevant in Europe despite the existence of tribes there as well, but which Europeans and others prefer to call ethnic groups to set them apart from "primitive" Africa. Or call it a clan like in Somalia. It is still a tribe in all its manifestations in terms of malignancy associated with tribalism.

Therefore countries like Kenya and Nigeria, Rwanda and Burundi, which have had serious ethnic conflicts ignited and fueled by power struggle between different groups, are not unique in this continent of polyethnic societies. They all face basically the same problems, but differ in the way they tackle them, if at all. In many cases, they do nothing.

But there are a few, in fact very few, exceptions where tribalism has not been a major problem in Africa. Tanzania is one of them.

Growing up in Tanganyika - later Tanzania - in the sixties was a unique experience in this part of Africa where many of our neighbors were going through turmoil, rocked by tribal conflicts and other forms of strife, during the very same time when we were enjoying relative peace and stability in my country.

The Hutu and the Tutsi in neighboring Rwanda and Burundi were at each other's throat, killing each other, a perennial problem in these two countries. The town of Kigoma, where I was born and which is on the shores of Lake Tanganyika, became a hub for refugee activities; and for decades the entire western region of Tanzania has been a sanctuary for refugees from Rwanda and Burundi as well as Congo.

The former Belgian Congo, another neighbor, was also torn by civil war, ignited and fueled by ethno-regional rivalries, secession, and intervention by outside powers including the United States and other Western countries especially Belgium, France, and apartheid South Africa as well as Rhodesia both of which also belonged to the Western camp. The Soviet Union and the People's Republic of China also intervened in the Congo.

All these highly combustible elements in one of Africa's biggest, potentially richest and most strategically located countries which slid into anarchy soon after independence on June 30, 1960, would have been too much for any leader to handle without solid national support for a strong central government. The Congo had neither.

The country was split along ethno-regional lines, making it impossible for any leader to mobilize national support for central authority. And the central government itself was weak, and national allegiance to it tenuous at best.

I remember listening to short-wave radio broadcasts from Congo's capital, Leopoldville (renamed Kinshasa by Mobutu in 1971), and from Elisabethville (now Lubumbashi), capital of the secessionist Katanga Province under Moise Tshombe which is about 300 miles west from my home province, Mbeya Region, on the Tanzania-Zambia-Malawi border in southwestern Tanzania. I was in Rungwe District then, in the Great Rift Valley, ringed by misty blue mountains in this region in the Southern Highlands of Tanzania.

The broadcasts were in Kiswahili, the national language of Tanzania and one of the languages spoken in Congo, and the war in that country dominated the news in the sixties. The Simba rebellion (*simba* means lion in Kiswahili), the capture of Stanleyville (now Kisangani) by Belgian paratroops with American support; the "disappearance" and subsequent assassination of Lumumba; the Kwilu rebellion led by Lumumba's heir-apparent Pierre Mulele and his subsequent assassination by Mobutu's henchmen (he was reportedly chopped up and his body pieces fed to crocodiles in the Congo River in October 1968); the battle for Katanga between Tshombe's army as well as mercenaries and the United Nations peacekeeping forces; these are some of the most memorable events I can easily recall even if I don't cherish the memory because of the devastation wrought in this bleeding heart of Africa.

Those were the turbulent sixties when the Congo was in the news everyday. Besides the radio broadcasts coming directly from Leopoldville and Elisabethville everyday about the war, we also got ample news about the same events on our national radio, TBC (Tanganyika Broadcasting Corporation), Dar es Salaam, later renamed RTD (Radio Tanzania, Dar es Salaam). The conflict in the Congo was one of the dominant stories even in Tanganyika, almost everyday. But there were other crises in the region.

Uganda, another neighbor of Tanzania and Congo, also had to contend with separatist threats by the Buganda kingdom; although not as serious as those in the Congo but serious enough to prompt Prime Minister Milton Obote to use military force to contain the danger. In May 1966, he swiftly deposed Kabaka (King) Edward

Frederick Mutesa II (who was Uganda's president, but only as nominal head) and declared a state of emergency in Buganda kingdom. And in June 1967, he abolished all four kingdoms and declared Uganda a republic. That was when he also became president.

The other traditional centers of power in the kingdoms of Toro, Ankole, and Bunyoro, and in the princedom of Busoga - as well as the region of Teso - had their own well-established political institutions like the Buganda kingdom and were equally suspicious of the national government which wanted to centralize power under a unitary state; thus stripping traditional rulers of authority over their own people. But they did not pose as big a threat to national unity as Kabaka Edward Mutesa did.

Another neighbor, Kenya, under the leadership of Mzee Jomo Kenyatta, had just emerged from Mau Mau, and the Kikuyu were consolidating their position as the dominant tribe across the spectrum at the expense of their rivals, the Luo, and other tribes; culminating in the assassination of 39-year-old Tom Mboya, a Luo and Kenyatta's heir-apparent, in July 1969.

I remember the day he was assassinated in broad daylight in Kenya's capital, Nairobi. It was Saturday afternoon, and I was at work then, as a reporter at the *Standard*, Dar es Salaam. The assassination is still vivid in my memory because of the magnitude of the tragedy itself. It was also one of the major assassinations in East Africa and, indeed, in the entire continent in the post-colonial era.

Tom Mboya's assassination threatened to plunge Kenya into chaos, a country already rife with ethnic tensions and rivalries. No one knew how members of his tribe, the Luo, and other Kenyans opposed to Kenyatta's leadership and domination by the Kikuyu, would react. Nashon Njenga Njoroge, a Kikuyu and the man arrested and accused of shooting Tom Mboya, said after he was captured: "Why don't you go after the big man?"

The implication of who exactly "the big man" was, besides Kenyatta himself and other Kikuyu political heavyweights of national stature such Mbiyu Koinange who was also close to Kenyatta, added to the confusion as tempers flared especially among the Luo, Mboya's fellow tribesmen. Large-scale violence was a distinct possibility.

Fortunately, nothing of the sort happened, much of this domestic tranquility attributed to Kenyatta's dominant personality as the revered father of the nation and to his tight grip on the nation he ruled with an iron fist.

But from then on, a cloud hung over Kenya, and prospects for peaceful co-existence between the country's two main ethnic groups and their allies remained bleak.

The problem was compounded by the mistreatment of Jaramogi Oginga Odinga, another prominent Luo politician of international stature who resigned as Kenya's vice president under Kenyatta and in March 1966 formed the opposition party, the Kenya People's Union (KPU). But he was effectively neutralized as an opposition leader.

His passport was withdrawn, preventing him from going to the United States in 1968 to deliver a lecture at Boston University, entitled, "Revolution As It Affects Newly Independent States." He was also denied permission to go to Tanzania where he had an ideological compatriot, President Julius Nyerere.

On October 27, 1969, Oginga Odinga was put under house arrest following an anti-government demonstration by KPU supporters and, three days later, the KPU was banned, leaving the Kenya African National Union (KANU) led by Kenyatta as the only legal party in the country. And on November 11, 1969, Kenyatta was re-elected to a second term. All this took place only about three months after Mboya was assassinated in July.

Yet, Oginga Odinga was one of Kenya's most revered politicians. He was also one of the most prominent leaders of the independence movement, not only in Kenya but in Africa as a whole. And it was he who led KANU when Kenyatta was in prison and could have very easily become Kenya's first president had he decided not to step aside when Kenyatta was released. It was also Oginga Odinga, together with Tom Mboya, who led the Kenyan delegation to the constitutional talks in London on Kenya's transition from colonial rule to independence.

Many Kenyans and others also remember him as the author of the best-selling book, *Not Yet Uhuru*,[3] meaning "Not Yet Freedom or Independence" (*uhuru* means freedom or independence in Kiswahili), which he wrote after he resigned as Kenya's vice president. President Julius Nyerere wrote the introduction to the book, as he did years later to that of President Yoweri Museveni who said he considers himself to be a disciple of Nyerere.

But although Odinga was silenced, he remained a highly respected leaders in Kenya. And he remains a revered figure in Kenyan politics even today on the same level with Kenyatta.

There were more crises in the region. In Zambia, formerly Northern Rhodesia before independence, just across the border from my home region in the Southern Highlands of Tanzania, violence also erupted on a significant scale. The country had just won independence from Britain on October 24, 1964, highly optimistic of the future under the leadership of Kenneth Kaunda, a former school teacher and an apostle of non-violence and author of a book, *Zambia Shall Be Free*.[4]

Yet, just before and after independence, the country was rocked by violence instigated by members of an anarchist independent church movement known as the Lumpa Church led by a prophetess, Alice Lenshina, which claimed hundreds of lives and disrupted the lives of thousands of people. The church members refused to pay taxes and rejected secular authority. They clashed with the government and fortified their villages, and refused to surrender to security forces. And they invoked the Scriptures to justify their defiance and refusal to submit to temporal authority.

The Lumpa Church and its leader Alice Lenshina became "household" names. And clashes between government forces and the church members was one of the major stories in the early sixties in that part of Africa, with the short-wave radio as an indispensable medium.

Zambia also had to contend with separatist threats in the western province, also known as Barotseland, which was and still is a powerful kingdom, and in the southern part of the country which was also the opposition stronghold of Zambia's main opposition leader Harry Nkumbula of the African National Congress (ANC).

Maluniko Mundia, leader of the United Party (UP), was another prominent opposition figure. He came from Barotse Province - Barotseland - where he was allied with the powerful traditional rulers including the king of the Barotse people. His party was banned in 1968 because of its sectarian politics, threatening national unity.

And just 30 miles from my home village of Mpumbuli in Kyimbila in the misty blue mountains of Rungwe District in the Great Rift Valley, across the border in Malawi (known as Nyasaland until July 6, 1966, when it won independence from Britain and changed its name), Life-President Dr. Hastings Kamuzu Banda had instituted a reign of terror, persecuting and killing his former compatriots, including leading cabinet members some of whom sought asylum in Tanzania.

They included Yatuta Chisiza, Malawi's former home affairs minister in Banda's cabinet, who was assassinated in October 1967 by security forces. Malawian officials claimed he entered the country from Tanzania in order to subvert the government with the help of the Tanzanian authorities.

Another one was Malawi's Minister of Foreign Affairs Kanyama Chiume who also sought asylum in Tanzania. When I was a reporter at the *Daily News* in Dar es Salaam, Kanyama Chiume was at *The Nationalist*, a daily newspaper owned by the ruling party TANU (Tanganyika African National Union), where he worked as a features writer and editor, together with Ben Mkapa who was the managing editor before President Nyerere appointed him editor of the *Daily News*. Years later, Mkapa himself was elected president of Tanzania for two five year-terms from 1995 to 2005.

Under Nyerere, Tanzania became a haven for asylum seekers and refugees from many African countries and others; and I attended Songea Secondary School in Ruvuma Region in the southern part of the country with some of the sons and relatives of these exiled cabinet members from Malawi, such as Henry Chipembere, who was minister of education under President Banda.

Other students at the school included the nephews of former Tanzanian Minister of Foreign Affairs Oscar Kambona who came from that region and who himself went into exile in Britain in July 1967 where he continued to be a fierce critic of Nyerere until his death in 1998, following his return to Tanzania in 1992 to form an opposition party after multiparty democracy was reintroduced that year.

And at our newspaper, the *Daily News*, we also had reporters from other countries including South Africa, Rhodesia (renamed Zimbabwe at independence in April 1980), Zambia, Kenya, Nigeria (from former Biafra), and Britain.

Dr. Banda also claimed substantial parts of Tanzania, including my home district - Rungwe - and the rest of Mbeya Region in southwestern Tanzania, as Malawian territory. He also claimed the entire Eastern Province of Zambia, provoking a curt response from Zambia's president, Dr. Kenneth Kaunda, who challenged Banda to "Go ahead and declare war on Zambia."[5]

And President Nyerere dismissed Banda's claim to large chunks of Tanzanian territory as "expansionist outbursts, which do not scare us, and do not deserve my reply." The outlandish claim also drew a sharp response from Nyerere who said Dr. Banda was "insane." But, he warned, "Dr. Banda must not be ignored; the powers behind him are not insane."[6]

So, that was the situation in these neighboring countries in the sixties when I was in my teens, and thereafter.

The situation in Mozambique, another neighbor, was somewhat different but equally explosive. Mozambique was still a Portuguese colony, and, because Tanzania gave full support to the freedom fighters who used our country as an operational base and headquarters of their liberation movement FRELIMO (Portuguese acronym for Mozambique Liberation Front), the Portuguese attacked parts of southern Tanzania, especially Mtwara Region, as well as Ruvuma Region where I attended Songea Secondary School from 1965 to 1968.

But the attacks only strengthened our resolve to support the freedom fighters; an unwavering commitment that continued until Mozambique finally won independence on June 25, 1975, after almost 500 years of Portuguese colonial rule.

One of the casualties of this liberation struggle was Dr. Eduardo Mondlane, founder and first president of FRELIMO, who was assassinated in Dar es Salaam in February 1969 when he opened a parcel, rigged with a bomb and mailed to him from Japan. The bomb, hidden in a book of Russian essays, was traced back to the Portuguese secret police in Lisbon.

I was then a student at Tambaza High School (formerly H.H. The Aga Khan High School) in Dar es Salaam. I was in standard 13 (Form V) that year. Our high school system had two grades, standard 13 and standard 14 (Form V and Form VI), covering two years, what Americans would call grade 13 and grade 14, after completion of secondary school in standard 12. This is roughly equivalent to what Americans call junior college, but with a concentration in three subjects, after which you went to university if you passed the dreaded final exams in standard 14. It was patterned after the British school system we inherited from our former colonial masters.

Many students, including myself, attended Mondlane's funeral at Kinondoni Cemetery within walking distance from our high school. President Nyerere was at the gravesite, together with Mondlane's widow Janet and their two little children, a boy and a girl. Leaders of all the African liberation movements based in Dar es Salaam and members of the diplomatic corps also attended the funeral, one of the saddest moments in our history.

But the assassination of Dr. Mondlane did not in any way interfere with the liberation struggle. President Nyerere, who had asked Mondlane to come to Tanganyika and establish an operational base in our country for the liberation of Mozambique when the two met at the United Nations where Mondlane worked and when Nyerere argued our case for Tanganyika's independence (he went to the UN for the first time in February 1955), vowed to continue supporting the freedom fighters until Mozambique was finally free.

Mondlane returned to Africa in 1962 and settled in Dar es Salaam, Tanganyika, where he went on to unite the various Mozambican nationalist groups to form FRELIMO, one of the most successful liberation movements in colonial history. Nyerere's invitation to the freedom fighters was typical of him. As he stated in his address to the Tanganyika Legislative Council (LEGCO) on October 22, 1959, even before our country became independent:

> We the people of Tanganyika, would like to light a candle and put it on top of Mount Kilimanjaro which would shine beyond our borders giving hope where there was despair, love where there was hate, and dignity where before there was only humiliation.[7]

And he went on to fulfill that pledge. Without Tanzania functioning as a rear base and as a conduit for material support to the freedom fighters, Mozambique would probably not have won independence when it did, and the liberation of other countries in southern Africa including the bastion of white rule on the continent, South Africa, would have been equally affected, only in varying degrees.

In spite of her poverty as one of the poorest countries in the world, Tanzania still contributed a significant amount of resources to the liberation struggle far more than many other and richer African countries did.

Many people used to say that Tazania contributed far more than its share; let other countries play their part. For instance, I remember talking to a Malawian surgeon, Dr. Geoffrey Mwaungulu, in Detroit, Michigan, in the United States when I was a student there in the early seventies, who said "Tanzania is doing too much," overburdening herself, while many other African countries - including his, Malawi - are doing nothing or very little to support the liberation struggle in southern Africa and Portuguese Guinea (Guinea-Bissau) in West Africa.

A graduate of Temple University in Philadelphia, Pennsylvania, he worked at Ford Hospital in Detroit and was one of a large number of African immigrants living in Detroit, including professors, lawyers, engineers and other professionals in that city and other parts of the metropolitan area.

There were even some people in Tanzania who said President Nyerere was devoting himself too much to the liberation struggle and pursuits of other foreign policy goals while overlooking domestic problems. Yet there was no contradiction between the two. His commitment to the well-being of Tanzania was not in any way compromised by the active role he played in the international arena.

And he could not have succeeded in the pursuit of his foreign policy objectives - including support of the liberation movements - without the unwavering support of the vast majority of Tanzanians. As David Martin, a renowned British journalist with *The Observer*, London, who was the deputy managing editor of the *Standard*, Tanzania, and the one who first hired me as a reporter in June 1969 when I was still a high school student, stated in December 2001, two years after Nyerere died:

I arrived in the Tanzanian capital of Dar es Salaam as a journalist on 9 January 1964. Three days later there was a revolution in Zanzibar by the African majority against the Arab minority put in power by the retreating British colonialists just one month earlier. An African-driven union between Tanganyika and Zanzibar followed three months later and the country's name was changed to Tanzania. Despair, hate and humiliation had begun the painfully slow process of retreating.

Dar es Salaam in those days was the headquarters of the Organization of African Unity (OAU) Liberation Committee. Living in the city were the leaders of the liberation movements of southern Africa such as the ebullient Eduardo Mondlane from Mozambique, more taciturn poet, Dr. Agostinho Neto, and a host of others. Nyerere was their beacon of hope.

He was uninhibited by the paranoid attitudes that gripped the east and west at the height of the Cold War. And although he was not adverse to using westerners to achieve his vision, he sought for the continent to have African solutions created by African people. He did not tolerate fools and was a masterly media manager. He could go for months without seeing the press. But, when he had something to say, as he did in 1976 during two visits by the US Secretary of State, Dr. Henry Kissinger, he astutely ensured that his version of events got across.

I remember one day sitting in his office questioning that a number of African countries had not paid their subscriptions to the OAU Liberation Committee Special Fund for the Liberation of Africa. He looked at me for some moments, thoughtfully chewing the inside corner of his mouth in his distinctive way. Then, his decision made, he passed across a file swearing me secrecy as to its contents. It contained the amount that Tanzanians, then according to the United Nations the poorest people on earth, would directly and indirectly contribute that year to the liberation movements. I was astounded; the amount ran into millions of US dollars.

It was the practice among national leaders in those days to say that their countries did not have guerrilla bases. Now we know that Tanzania had many such bases providing training for most of the southern African guerrillas, who were then called 'terrorists' and who today are members of governments throughout the region.... Tanzania was also directly attacked from Mozambique by the Portuguese. But, in turn, each of the white minorities in southern Africa fell to black majority political rule and Nyerere saw his vision for the continent finally realized on 27 April 1994 when apartheid formally ended in South Africa with the swearing in of a new black leadership.[8]

Mozambique was the first country in the region to win independence by armed struggle, six years after Dr. Mondlane was assassinated. His assassination in February 1969 was one of the two major political killings in the region that year, followed by the assassination of Tom Mboya only a few months later in July, about a month after I was first hired as a news reporter of the

Standard, renamed *Daily News* in 1970. I started working full-time on the editorial staff in 1971 after completing high school and National Service.

As a reporter, I used to go to the headquarters of the Mozambique Liberation Front, FRELIMO, on Nkrumah Street in Dar es Salaam for the latest developments on the guerrilla war in Mozambique and to pick up press releases. The office of the African National Congress (ANC) of South Africa was also on the same street, on the opposite side, not far from FRELIMO's, just a few minutes' walk, probably not more than five minutes. The person I always spoke to when I went to FRELIMO's office was Joaquim Chissano who became president of Mozambique after the tragic death of President Samora Machel in a plane crash in October 1986.

President Machel and his entourage were on their way back to Mozambique from Harare, Zimbabwe, when the plane crashed just inside the South African border not far from Maputo, the Mozambican capital. The South African government was immediately implicated in the crash, and subsequent investigations showed that the "accident" was an act of sabotage by the apartheid regime.

The South African government was also behind the assassination of Swedish Prime Minister Olof Palme on February 28, 1986. Palme, who was shot by a gunman as he was walking home with his wife from a movie theater, was a strong supporter of the African liberation movements in southern Africa, as was his country, which - especially under his leadership - reportedly contributed more than $400 million to the liberations struggle in terms of financial and non-military support.

Chissano was in charge of the FRELIMO office in Dar es Salaam, and became Mozambique's minister of foreign affairs after his country won independence. He held the same ministerial post until he became president after Samora Machel was killed. Marcelino dos Santos who also used to live in Tanzania during the struggle for Mozambique's independence, remained vice president, under Chissano, as he was under Samora Machel.

Our interaction with the FRELIMO office in Dar es Salaam as reporters was facilitated by Chissano because he also spoke English, besides Portuguese. He also learned and spoke Kiswahili, our national language. So, it was easy for us to communicate with him, as much as it was with most of the freedom fighters from other countries at their headquarters in Dar es Salaam who also spoke English, and some of them Kiswahili.

Dar es Salaam during those days was the center of seismic activity on the African political landscape and beyond. The list of the names of those who came to the city, who lived there, and those who just passed through during the liberation wars, is highly impressive to say the least. It was here, in Tanzania, where Nelson Mandela first came in 1962 to seek assistance for the liberation struggle in South Africa. And Nyerere was the first leader of independent Africa he met.

Tanganyika was also the first country in the region to win independence, in 1961. Mandela also had his first taste of freedom after he arrived in Mbeya, a border town in southwestern Tanzania (then Tanganyika) and the capital of the Southern Highlands Province (later split into Mbeya and Iringa Regions) where, as he states in his autobiography *Long Walk to Freedom*, he was not - for the first time in his life - subjected to the indignities of color bar as he automatically would been in his native land.9

Almost all the leaders in southern Africa who waged guerrilla warfare to free their countries from white minority rule, lived or worked in Tanzania at one time or another.

Thabo Mbeki, who became vice president and then president of South Africa, first sought asylum in Tanganyika when he fled the land of apartheid in the early sixties. So did others, including many leaders in South Africa today besides Mbeki. They include the Speaker of the South African Parliament Dr. Frene Ginwala who once was editor of our newspaper, the *Daily News*, appointed by President Nyerere before Sammy Mdee replaced her. She lived in Tanzania for many years and is the person who received Mandela in Dar es Salaam when he first came to Tanganyika in 1962.

President Robert Mugabe also lived in Tanzania and Mozambique during Zimbabwe's liberation war. So did Dr. Agostinho Neto, the first president of Angola, and Sam Nujoma, president of Namibia, and many of their colleagues in government.

I remember interviewing Sam Nujoma in 1972 at the office of his liberation movement, the South West African People's Organization (SWAPO), on Market Street in Dar es Salaam, only a few minutes' walk from our newspaper office on Azikiwe Street and from the offices of three other liberation movements: Zimbabwe African National Union (ZANU), Popular Movement for the Liberation of Angola (MPLA), and the Pan-Africanist Congress (PAC) of South Africa. I talked to Nujoma just before he left for New York to address the United Nations Decolonization Committee and speak in other forums in his quest for Namibian independence.

Looking very serious, and highly articulate on the subject, he was very optimistic about the future. He was, of course, vindicated by history. But little did he or anybody else back then know that it would be almost 20 years before Namibia would be free.

Many other leaders found sanctuary in Tanzania. They include those from the Seychelles and the Comoros, two island nations on the Indian Ocean east and southeast of Tanzania, respectively; and President Yoweri Museveni of Uganda who attended the University of Dar es Salaam and lived in Tanzania for many years and who - after he became president - continued to express profound respect and admiration for Nyerere whom he acknowledged as his mentor.[7]

When he was a student at the University of Dar es Salaam, Museveni was a member of a study group led by Dr. Walter Rodney. Mwalimu Nyerere even wrote an introduction to one of President Museveni's books, *What Is Africa's Problem?*[10]

The late President Laurent Kabila of the Democratic Republic of Congo also lived in Tanzania for more than 20 years since the sixties after the assassination of Patrice Lumumba, his hero, and even owned houses in Dar es Salaam where he was also known by different aliases, prompting his neighbors and other people to suspect that he was a government agent.

His son Joseph Kabila who succeeded him as president was born and brought up in Tanzania. He also attended school in Tanzania. In fact, many Congolese refused to accept him as their leader soon after he succeeded his father – and even after the presidential election in 2006 - because they saw him as a foreigner, a Tanzanian, who did not even speak Lingala or French, the main languages spoken in Congo, but instead spoke only English and Kiswahili, Tanzania's national language, although Kiswahili is also widely spoken in Congo.

And in the 2006 presidential election, the first democratic election since the Congo won independence from Belgium in 1960, he won overwhelming support in the eastern half of the country where the people speak Swahili or Kiswahil; a language that virtually unites that region with Tanzania where Kabila spent most of his life. His rival Jean-Pierre Mbembe won overwhelming in western Congo where the people speak Lingala as the lingua franca.

Both Kabilas, the father and the son, were just some of the leaders of national stature who had strong ties to Tanzania.

President Kenneth Kaunda of Zambia also forged ties with Tanzania early in his life.

He spent some time in Mbeya in the southwestern part of what was then Tanganyika, and with his friend Simon Kapwepwe who also spent some time in Mbeya and later became his vice president, used to dream of the day when Northern Rhodesia (Zambia) would be free one day. The two were childhood friends in Chinsali - their hometown and district in the Northern Province - in Northern Rhodesia renamed Zambia.

The list of people who found asylum in Tanzania goes on and on. They include many who became leaders in Rwanda, Burundi, Ethiopia, Eritrea, Somalia, Sudan, Ghana, Nigeria, Guinea, Congo, Zambia, besides those in southern Africa - Mozambique, Zimbabwe, Angola, Namibia, South Africa - and other countries. There were also many non-Africans who were attracted to Tanzania when Nyerere was president.

Che Guevara was one of them. He spent months in Tanzania. He was in Dar es Salaam for about four months from November 1965 to February 1966, besides the time he spent in the western apart of the country during his Congo mission. And it was when he was in Dar es Salaam that he wrote his famous book, the *Congo Diaries*,[11] while staying at the Cuban embassy during those critical months.

In fact, before he embarked on his Congo mission, it was Che Guevara himself who recommended Pablo Ribalta - his friend and compatriot since their guerrilla war days in the Sierra Maestra during the Cuban revolution - to be Cuba's ambassador to Tanzania because he felt that Ribalta's African ancestry would facilitate his mission to the Congo.

And during his military engagement in the Congo, Che sometimes used Kigoma in western Tanzania as one of his sanctuaries. But he had a very low opinion of Laurent Kabila - whom he said had no leadership qualities and lacked charisma - and other Congolese nationalist leaders including Gaston-Emile Sumayili Sumialot. He accused them of abandoning their troops in eastern Congo preferring, instead, to live in comfort in Dar es Salaam.

But in spite of the fact that Tanzania was the headquarters of all the African liberation movements and a place which attracted many liberals and leftists from many parts of the world including black militants from the United States such as the Black Panthers (among them Black Panther leader Pete O'Neal and his wife Charlotte who have lived in Tanzania since 1972), and Malcolm X who also visited Tanzania and had a meeting with President Nyerere and attended the OAU conference of the African heads of state and government in Cairo, Egypt, in July 1964 (where he almost died when his food was poisoned, probably by CIA agents who followed him throughout his African trip); our country still enjoyed relative peace and stability, not only during the euphoric sixties soon after independence, but also during the seventies when the liberation wars were most intense in southern Africa, with Dar es Salaam, our capital, as the nerve center.

Therefore, besides the raids by the Portuguese from their colony of Mozambique on our country; a sustained destabilization campaign by the apartheid regime of South Africa whose Defence Minister P.W. Botha said in August 1968 that countries which harbor terrorists - freedom fighters in our lexicon - should receive "a sudden knock,"[12] a pointed reference to Tanzania and Zambia, and by the white minority government of Rhodesia (Prime Minister Ian Smith called Nyerere "the evil genius" behind the liberation wars), all of whom had singled out Tanzania as the primary target because of our support for the freedom fighters; the influx of refugees from Rwanda, Burundi, and Congo into our country; and Malawian President Banda's claims to our territory;

in spite of all that, Tanzania was, relatively speaking, not only an island of peace and stability in the region but also an ideological center with considerable magnetic pull, drawing liberal and radical thinkers from around the world, especially to the University of Dar es Salaam which became one of the most prominent academic centers in the world with many internationally renowned scholars who strongly admired Nyerere and his policies.

Among the scholars drawn to Tanzania was the late Dr. Walter Rodney from Guyana who first joined the academic staff at the University of Dar es Salaam in 1968 and, while teaching there, wrote a best-seller, *How Europe Underdeveloped Africa*;[13] the late distinguished Professor Claude Ake from Nigeria who died in a mysterious plane crash in his home country in 1996; Professor Okwudiba Nnoli, also from Nigeria (secessionist Biafra); Professor Mahmood Mamdani from Uganda and one of Africa's internationally renowned scholars; Nathan Shamuyarira who - while a lecturer at the University of Dar es Salaam - was also the leader of the Dar-es-Salaam-based Front for the Liberation of Zimbabwe (FROLIZI) headed by James Chikerema, a Zimbabwean national leader. Shamuyarira went on to become Zimbabwe's minister of foreign affairs, among other ministerial posts he held.

Many other prominent scholars from many countries around the world, and from all continents, were also attracted to the University of Dar es Salaam. C.L.R. James from Trinidad & Tobago, one of the founding fathers of the Pan-Africanist movement who knew Kwame Nkrumah when Nkrumah was still a student in the United States, and who introduced him to George Padmore when Nkrumah went to Britain for further studies before returning to Ghana (then the Gold Coast) in 1947 with Ako Adjei, was also attracted to Tanzania. So was Kenyan writer Ngugi wa Thiong'o, disenchanted with the Kenyan leadership, and Ghanaian writer Ayi Kwei Armah, an admirer of Nkrumah and Nyerere, who has also called for the adoption of Kiswahili as the continental language just as Wole Soyinka has.

Besides Malcolm X, other prominent black American leaders who came to Tanzania included Stokely Carmichael (originally from Trinidad) who as Kwame Ture lived in Guinea for 30 years until his death in November 1998. When in Dar es Salaam, Stokely used to stay at the Palm Beach Hotel, not far from the Indian Ocean beach and our high school hostel, H.H. The Aga Khan, in an area called Upanga; while Malcolm X and Che Guevara used to go to the New Zahir restaurant. But while Malcolm X was in Tanzania only for days, Che spent about four months in Dar es Salaam.

Angela Davis of the Black Panther Party and others in the civil rights movement including Andrew Young, Jesse Jackson, and Robert Williams who organized some blacks for self-defense in North Carolina, also came to Tanzania.

I also remember when Robert Williams came to our editorial office at the *Daily News* in Dar es Salaam. I saw him again in 1975 when I was a student at Wayne State University in Detroit, Michigan, USA. He came to Detroit and spoke to Wayne State University students who were members of the Young Socialist Alliance (YSA). He lived in Baldwin, Michigan, during that time and in the following years.

I was at that meeting as an observer and reminded him of his visit to our newspaper office in Tanzania, which he remembered very well, as we went on to talk about a number of subjects including the influence of President Nyerere in a Pan-African context. He died in 1996.

Some of the prominent leaders in the American civil rights movement who lived in Tanzania for a number of years include Charlie Cobb and Robert (Bob) Moses. They were active in Mississippi and other parts of the Deep South during the turbulent sixties when they almost got killed. Bob Moses was one of those who got a thorough beating in Mississippi for trying to organize blacks to vote. The White Citizens Council, founded in Greenville in Mississippi, the Ku Klux Klan and other racist groups could not tolerate that. Cobb had similar close calls. Both eventually moved to Africa. After they returned to the United States, they continued to be involved in civil rights activities and organizing communities for their collective well-being.

They co-authored *Radical Equations: Math Literacy and Civil Rights* and developed an algebra curriculum also designed to mobilize communities to achieve common goals. Launched in 1982, the Algebra Project now operates in many cities and communities across the United States, and their book, *Radical Equations*, describes the project's creation and implementation. The project involves entire communities to create a culture of literacy around algebra, a crucial stepping-stone to college math and opportunity, especially for blacks and other minorities who lag behind in preparation for college work because of the low quality of education they get in inner-city schools.

Bob Moses, who was a secondary school teacher in Tanzania, began developing the Algebra Project after becoming unhappy with the way algebra was taught to his teen-age daughter. He saw algebra as a major obstacle for black students trying to go to college.

Charlie Cobb was a field secretary for the Student Non-violent Coordinating Committee (SNNC), once headed by Stokely Carmichael, in Mississippi from 1962 to 1967 where he developed the idea for the Freedom Schools that SNNC operated. The schools taught basic literacy skills to black children and became a model for many new approaches to education still used today across the United States.

He also helped found the National Association for Black Journalists and became a senior writer for allafrica.com, the web site of AllAfrica Global Media. The site posts hundreds of news stories about Africa everyday from more than 80 African media organizations and its own reporters.

The years the two civil rights activists and many others spent in Tanzania helped strengthen ties between Africa and Black America, and is strong testimony to Tanzania's hospitality to oppressed people from around the world who found sanctuary in Tanzania during Nyerere's tenure.

The relationship between Tanzania and Black America has also been demonstrated in many other ways. For example, when Malcolm X returned to the United States from Africa, FBI agents were waiting for him at the airport in New York. He was seen going into a car with a diplomatic license plate which was traced to "the new African nation of Tanzania." The car took him to the residence of the Tanzanian ambassador to the United Nations, trailed by FBI agents the same way Malcolm X was followed by CIA agents throughout his African trip.

President Nyerere also forged ties with Black America soon

after independence when he instructed the Tanzanian ambassador to the United States to recruit skilled African-Americans to work in Tanzania to help the country meet its manpower requirements and as act of Pan-African solidarity.

There are also schools and other institutions in black communities in the United States named after Nyerere and other African leaders such as Nkrumah, Lumumba and Mandela. And Kiswahili, Tanzania's national language, is the most popular African language among African-Americans; much of this popularity attributed to the influence and stature of Mwalimu Julius Nyerere as an eminent Pan-Africanist who was embraced by the African diaspora as much as Nkrumah was. Many African-Americans came to Tanzania because of Nyerere and his policies. Others viewed their trip as a pilgrimage, a spiritual journey, and a return to the motherland in the spirit of Pan-African solidarity.

One of the African-Americans who was among the earliest to settle in Africa was Bill Sutherland, like Dr. W.E.B. DuBois and George Padmore, both of whom he knew and worked with in Ghana where they also lived and died. He came from Glen Ridge, New Jersey, and lived in Tanzania for decades. He knew and worked with Nyerere and was still in Tanzania when Nyerere died. Influenced by Mahatma Gandhi as a youth, he became a pacifist and worked for the Quaker-affiliated American Friends Service Committee after he graduated from Bates College in Maine. From 1942 to 1945, he was in a federal penitentiary as a war resister.

He first went to Africa in 1953 and settled in Ghana where he worked closely with Kwame Nkrumah. And through the years, he met or worked with many other African leaders including Nyerere, Kaunda, Lumumba, Tom Mboya, Mandela; others in the diaspora such as Frantz Fanon, and Malcolm X whom he interviewed extensively; as well as the leaders of the liberation movements in southern Africa, all of whom were based in Tanzania.

In his book he wrote with Matt Mayer, *Guns and Gandhi in Africa: Pan-African Insights on Nonviolence, Armed Struggle and Liberation in Africa*, Sutherland has a lot to say about Nyerere whom he knew and worked with for more than 30 years. He moved to Tanganyika after he fell out with Nkrumah and left

Ghana following his criticism of Nkrumah's increasing dictatorial tendencies and abandonment of nonviolence in the struggle for African liberation.

When he settled in Dar es Salaam, he became involved in politics - as he had always been - and worked in the office of Prime Minister Rashidi Kawawa who became vice president of Tanganyika under Nyerere, and later second vice-president of Tanzania; with the president of Zanzibar, Abeid Karume, serving as first vice-president as stipulated by the constitution of the United Republic of Tanzania.

As with Nkrumah, Bill Sutherland also disagreed with Nyerere on the same subject of non-violence and quotes him in his book. As Nyerere explained his support for armed struggle to liberate southern Africa: "When you win, the morale of the African freedom fighters will go up and the morale of their opponents throughout southern Africa will go down. I said that's what we should do, demonstrate success, which we did."

Sutherland also quotes Nyerere as saying that although the struggle for Tanganyika's independence was non-violent, he was not opposed to the use of violence if that was the only way to win freedom. Therefore his opposition to violence or support of armed struggle was not based on principle but dictated by circumstances. As Nyerere told Sutherland about the non-violent struggle for Tanganyika's independence: "The nonviolence of our movement was not philosophical at all...My opposition to violence is [to] the unnecessary use of violence."

And Zambian President Dr. Kenneth Kaunda, once a pacifist himself, asked Sutherland and co-author Matt Meyer if they had ever run a country on pacifist principles. As he put it: "Have you tried running a country on the basis of pacifist principles without qualification or modification, or do you know anyone who has?" As Sutherland states in the book, the discussion went well into the night, "but the upshot was that nobody had a clear and definable answer. We were not really able to respond to Kaunda."

I remember talking to Bill Sutherland in Grand Rapids, Michigan, USA, in the summer of 1977 when he spoke about the liberation struggle in southern Africa. He also talked about other African subjects including Idi Amin, saying Amin did what he did in many cases just "for a little bit of publicity," as he put it. He also happened to know well some of the people, including national leaders, I knew in Tanzania.

I was still a student then, in the United States, following closely the events in Africa including the liberation wars in southern Africa. We agreed on almost everything except the armed struggle. I supported it. But even he as a pacifist was ambivalent about it, especially in the context of southern Africa.

He understood the necessity of armed struggle but, as a pacifist, could not as a matter of principle support the use of violence. I saw it as the only viable option; a concession he grudgingly made in conversations with the freedom fighters in Tanzania and elsewhere, and even with Nyerere and Kaunda, although they also agreed to disagree. Yet he also realized that he could not really oppose the use of violence in southern Africa, considering the nature of the situation.

Nor could he justify the use of non-violence in a situation where the oppressor did not have the slightest compunction shooting and killing unarmed, defenseless, and innocent men, women and children for no other reason than that they were demanding basic human rights, including the sanctity of life pacifists themselves invoke to justify non-violence.

Yet, he was a dedicated Pan-Africanist who made Tanzania his home, a country which became the most relentless supporter of armed struggle in southern Africa. And he settled in Tanzania because of Julius Nyerere who was already, even back then in the 1950s, becoming increasingly influential in African affairs, especially in the liberation of our continent from colonialism and imperialism.

A number of revolutionary thinkers from Latin America, Europe, and Asia were equally drawn to Tanzania and lived in Dar es Salaam which was the center of ideological ferment and provided an environment conducive to cross-fertilization of ideas stimulated by Nyerere's policies and ideological leadership.

And Tanzania's prominent role in the African liberation struggle and world affairs because of Nyerere's leadership put the country in a unique position on a continent where few governments looked beyond their borders, with most of them content to pursue goals in the narrow context of "national interest," which really meant securing and promoting the interests of the leaders themselves.

Tanzania was therefore an anomaly in that sense, on the continent, as a haven and an incubator for activists and revolutionaries from around the world. And it remained that way as a magnet throughout Nyerere's tenure. It was also his leadership more than anything else, which played a critical role in forging and shaping the identity of our nation and in enabling Tanzania to play an important role on the global scene, far beyond its wealth and size, especially in promoting the interests of Africa and the Third World in general.

The fact that Nyerere himself was chosen as chairman of the South Commission, a forum for action and dialogue between the poor and the rich countries on how to address problems of economic inequalities in a global context, is strong testimony to that. And it was in this crucible of identity, a country that would not be what it is today had it not been for Nyerere that my own personality was shaped.

In some fundamental respects, it is an identity and an ethos like no other on the continent: an indigenous national language, Kiswahili, transcending tribalism and not claimed by any particular ethnic group as its own - all the tribes and racial minorities contributed to its creation and growth, a unique phenomenon; social equality as an egalitarian ideal implemented by Nyerere through the decades; national unity - and stability - that has virtually eliminated tribalism and racism as major problems in national life, and in a country where speaking tribal languages in front of other people who don't understand those languages is frowned upon.

Kiswahili helped Tanzania's 126 different tribes and racial minorities - Arab, Asian, mostly of Indian and Pakistani origin, and European - to develop a sense of national unity and identity which has remained solid through the years regardless of what the country has undergone since independence in 1961. And the egalitarian policies of President Nyerere reduced social inequalities across the nation and guaranteed equal access to health, education, and other services on a scale unequalled anywhere else on the continent.

But probably more than any other asset, it was Nyerere's leadership which proved to be most useful at a time when we needed it most to forge a true sense of national identity, maintain national stability, and consolidate our independence; as much as Mandela's magnanimity and wisdom proved to be an indispensable asset in South Africa's transition from apartheid to democracy at a time when the country could have exploded, engulfing it in a racial conflagration. The pundits and laymen alike who predicted this were proved wrong largely because of Mandela's astute leadership, like Nyerere's.

Therefore it's not surprising that they are the only two African leaders who are favorably compared to each other with equal international and moral stature - hence Nyerere's honorific title, "The Conscience of Africa." There is nobody else in their league.

I remember Nyerere well. Cordially known as Mwalimu, which means Teacher in Kiswahili, he led by example; his humility equalled by his commitment to the well-being of the poorest of the poor, yet without ignoring the rights of others. And he asked all to make sacrifices for our collective well-being. As he put it, "It can be done. Play your part."

His dedication and identification with the masses, and his passion for fairness, were evident throughout his tenure as the nation's leader. When he became president, he worked and lived with them in their villages, slept in their huts, and ate their food. He spent days, and weeks, working with them in the rural areas in all parts of the country. He mingled with the peasants so well that you wouldn't even know who the leader was in the group, let alone be able to identify him as president of a country if you didn't know how he looked like. I know this because I worked as a news reporter in Tanzania.

No other African leader lived the way he did, and worked in the rural areas as much as he did, clearing and tilling the land for hours with ordinary peasants. He was one of them and, they said, "He's one of us." Not a detached, arrogant leader and intellectual who felt it was beneath him to soil his hands like the poor, illiterate peasants did. I also know how humble he was, because of what I witnessed years before I even became a national news reporter, first at the *Standard*, next at the Ministry of Information and Broadcasting as an information officer, and then at the *Daily News*.

I remember Nyerere when he was campaigning for

independence. It was in the late 1950s when I first saw him. He had already been to the United States, and even appeared on American television with Eleanor Roosevelt in 1956 when he was interviewed by Mike Wallace, a prominent American television journalist and interviewer who was still on the air in 2006, although in his eighties.

Nyerere went to the United States to present our case for independence at the United Nations where he appeared more than once in the late fifties, and before American audiences including academic gatherings such as the one at Wellesley College in Massachusetts in 1960 where he participated in a symposium and delivered a lecture, "Africa and the World."

I was just a little boy then, under ten, when he came to our home district in the late fifties more than once. I first saw him around 1958. He was about 36 years old. But in spite of my age - I was born on 4 October 1949 - what I saw then remains vivid in my memory as if it happened only yesterday.

I was a pupil at Kyimbila Primary School, about two miles from Tukuyu. Founded by the German colonial rulers and named Neu Langenburg, Tukuyu was our district headquarters for Rungwe District. The town was destroyed by earthquakes in 1910 and 1919 but was rebuilt. It had been the district headquarters since the German colonial rulers built it when they first came to the area in the early 1890s.

When the British took over Tanganyika - then known as German East Africa which included Rwanda and Burundi as one colony - after the Germans lost World War I, they continued the tradition and kept the town (whose name was changed from Neu Langenburg to Tukuyu) as the headquarters of Rungwe District headed by a British District Commissioner, simply known as DC, who lived there.

Nyerere came to Tukuyu one afternoon and our head teacher, who also happened to be a relative of mine, led us on a trip from our school to Tukuyu to listen to him. As life was then, and as it still is today across Africa for most people including children, we walked the two miles to Tukuyu to hear him speak; a man who, we were told, was our leader and who was going to be president of Tanganyika in only about three years, replacing the British governor.

I was then too young to understand the complexities of politics and political campaigning all of which to us at that age seemed to be expressed in esoteric terms. Yet we were old enough to understand what Nyerere was saying in general; a message delivered in his usual simple style everybody, including children my age, was able to understand. And he knew there were children at the rally. He saw us.

He arrived in an open Land Rover, standing in the back, waving at the crowd. The people were just as jubilant. He stepped out of the Land Rover and walked to the football (soccer) field to address the mass rally. He wore a simple short-sleeved light-green shirt and a pair of long trousers (pants), and started speaking, using a megaphone.

It was a cloudy afternoon and, after he spoke for only a few minutes, it started raining. The leading local politician of the Tanganyika African National Union (TANU), Mr. Mwambenja, a formidable personality and relentless campaigner for independence, who welcomed Nyerere at the rally tried to hold an umbrella over him. But he refused to accept it and continued to speak.

He even joked about himself implying that he was a non-entity, an insignificant personality, and said something to the effect that the colonialists and other detractors were now, with all that rain saying, "Just let him get soaked and washed away."

The subtle message in this self-deprecating humor was that he was not going to fade into oblivion and give up the struggle for independence. And it kept on raining. But the rain did not dampen his spirits. We also stayed as almost everybody else did, impressed by his humility and simplicity despite his status as the most prominent and acknowledged leader of Tanganyika, besides the British governor Sir Edward Twining who was later succeeded by Sir Richard Turnbull, the last governor. He got soaked in the rain just like the rest of us and continued to speak until he finished addressing the rally.

It was such humility, devotion and simplicity, which remained the hallmark of his life and leadership. And it was evident even among some members of his family.

I attended school with his eldest son, Andrew, at Tambaza High School, the former H.H. The Aga Khan High School which had been exclusively for students of Asian origin, mostly Indian and Pakistani, almost all of whom were Tanzanians. There were also some Arab students. And there were only a few of us, black students. We were among the first to integrate the school as mandated by the government under Nyerere. In fact, Mwalimu himself had experienced racial discrimination, what we in East Africa - and elsewhere including southern Africa - also call color bar. As Colin Legum states in a book he edited with Tanzanian Professor Geoffrey Mmari, *Mwalimu: The Influence of Nyerere:*

> I was privileged to meet Nyerere while he was still a young teacher in short trousers at the very beginning of his political career, and to engage in private conversations with him since the early 1950s.
> My very first encounter in 1953 taught me something about his calm authority in the face of racism in colonial Tanganyika. I had arranged a meeting with four leaders of the nascent nationalist movement at the Old Africa Hotel in Dar es Salaam.
> We sat at a table on the pavement and ordered five beers, but before we could lift our glasses an African waiter rushed up and whipped away all the glasses except mine. I rose to protest to the white manager, but Nyerere restrained me. 'I am glad it happened,' he said, 'now you can go and tell your friend Sir Edward Twining [the governor at the time] how things are in this country.' His manner was light and amusing, with no hint of anger.[14]

Simple, yet profound. For, beneath the surface lay a steely character with a deep passion for justice across the color line and an uncompromising commitment to the egalitarian ideals he espoused and implemented throughout his political career, favoring none.

Years later his son, Andrew Nyerere, told me about an incident that also took place in the capital Dar es Salaam shortly after Tanganyika won independence. Like the incident earlier when Julius Nyerere was humiliated at the Old Africa Hotel back in 1953, this one also involved race. As Andrew said in a letter to me in 2003 when I was writing this book:

> As you remember, Sheikh Amri Abeid was the first mayor of Dar es Salaam.
> Soon after independence, the mayor went to Palm Beach Hotel (near our high school, Tambaza, in Upanga). There was a sign at the hotel which clearly stated: 'No Africans and dogs allowed inside.'
> He was blocked from entering the hotel, and said in protest, 'But I am the

Mayor.' Still he was told, 'You will not get in.' Shortly thereafter, the owner of the hotel was given 48 hours to leave the country.

When the nationalization exercise began, that hotel was the first to be nationalized.

Such insults were the last thing that could be tolerated in newly independent Tanganyika. And President Nyerere, probably more than any other African leader, would not have tolerated, and did not tolerate, seeing even the humblest of peasants being insulted and humiliated by anyone including fellow countrymen.

And his passion for equality was legendary. For example, he sent his son Andrew to a local school - with the sons of peasants and workers - when he could have sent him abroad, as was customary among most leaders across the continent. They either sent their children to exclusively private and expensive schools within their own countries, or flew them overseas, and still do.

All this was in keeping with his commitment to social equality for all Tanzanians. He said we are not going to build a society based on privilege; we are going to narrow the gap between the haves and the have-nots, and abolish classes which accentuate cleavages and define some human beings as better than others. At our high school, many people knew that President Nyerere's eldest son was one of the students. Yet he got no special favors. He was treated just like the rest of us, and we saw him as just another student like us.

And he saw himself that way, and acted that way. You wouldn't even know he was the president's son because of the way he behaved and carried himself, just as an ordinary student, and the way the rest of us treated him. We lived in the same hostel, most of whose students were Tanzanians of Asian origin; ate the same food at the same table, and worked on the farm together, tilling the land, as true sons of a nation of peasants and workers.

Our school in Dar es Salaam had a farm near Muhimbili National Hospital where we were required to work to instill egalitarian values in our minds. We walked to the farm, about two miles round trip, carrying hoes and sickles and other agricultural implements; a strong reminder that we were no better than ordinary peasants and workers simply because we had acquired some education and were destined to become part of the nation's elite.

And Nyerere's son also walked around the city with fellow students and other friends, just like the rest of us, when many people would probably have expected him as the president's son to ride in a Mercedes Benz. But that was not the kind of society based on class and privilege President Nyerere was trying to build. And to his son's credit, he was just as humble and friendly with everybody.

Mwalimu Nyerere did not even force his children to toe the party line. One of his sons, Charles Makongoro - different from another Makongoro who attended school with us at Tambaza and who was sometimes mistaken for President Nyerere's son - left the ruling party founded by his father and, with the blessings of his family, joined what was then the country's leading opposition party on Tanzania mainland; the Civic United Front (CUF) was the main opposition party in Zanzibar, not on the mainland, as it still is today.

In 1995, Charles Makongoro Nyerere was elected as one of the few opposition members of parliament, but lost his seat following a court ruling before his five-year term expired. He then rejoined the ruling party. He returned to parliament in February 2004 after President Benjamin Mkapa appointed him a member; one of the 10 members the president is empowered to appoint to the national legislature at his discretion as stipulated by the constitution of the United Republic of Tanzania.

And in 2005, Nyerere's eldest son, Andrew, also joined one of the opposition parties, the Tanganyika Labour Party (TLP). When the party's leader Augustine Mrema asked him - at the party's meeting in Dar es Salaam where he was given a membership card - to denounce the ruling party, CCM (Chama Cha Mapinduzi - the Revolutionary Party), once led by his father, Andrew said he could not do that since he had never been a member of CCM. CCM was formed as a merger of TANU (Tanganyika African National Union), the mainland ruling party, and the Afro-Shirazi Party (ASP) of Zanzibar. Although Andrew never joined CCM, I remember that he was a member of the TANU Youth League when we were together at Tambaza High School.

Our school was also fully integrated. We lived in the same hostel with Asian and Arab students. We also had African, Asian and European teachers, most of them Tanzanian citizens. Other schools across Tanzania were also fully integrated - student and faculty. At our school, students came from all parts of the country and from many different tribes.

We were not encouraged to attend school - except at the primary school level - in our home districts, which were usually inhabited by members of our own tribes. We were, in fact, assigned to schools and jobs after graduation far away from our tribal homelands in order to live and work with members of other tribes. It was a deliberate effort by the government to break down barriers between members of different tribes and races in order to achieve national unity. And it worked.

This was probably Nyerere's biggest achievement - the creation of a cohesive political entity unique on a continent rife with ethnic tensions and torn by conflict caused and fueled by ethno-regional rivalries in the struggle for power and for the nation's resources.

Our schools were a microcosm of what Tanzania became: a united, integrated, peaceful and stable nation.

It was also when I was in high school at Tambaza that I first got hired in June 1969 as a reporter by the *Standard*, which became the *Daily News* the following year. I started working full-time in 1971 after I finished high school (Form VI or standard 14) the previous year.

Our managing editor was Brendon Grimshaw, a British, and the news and deputy editor was David Martin, also British, who also worked for the London *Observer* for many years after he left Tanzania. David Martin also worked for the BBC and even covered the Angolan civil war. I remember listening to him in a live report from Angola on the CBC (Canadian Broadcasting Corporation, Toronto) radio when I lived in Detroit, Michigan, USA, in the seventies.

President Nyerere was our editor-in-chief. But he never served in an executive capacity at the *Daily News*. As an overall guardian of this publicly owned institution - the paper, the *Standard*, was renamed *Daily News* in 1970 when it was nationalized - he gave us the freedom to say what we wanted to say and even encouraged us to criticize the government and its policies. And he meant what he said.

We wrote what we wanted to write without any fear of retribution or censorship. Others also testify to that. As Philip Ochieng', probably Kenya's best known journalist and political commentator who was attracted to Tanzania by Nyerere's leadership and policies and who joined our editorial staff at the *Daily News*, stated in a tribute to Mwalimu, "There Was Real Freedom in Mwalimu's Day," in *The East African*:

> I never really covered Mwalimu Nyerere. By the time I got to Tanzania to work for *The Standard Tanzania*, I had been an editorial pontiff in Nairobi's *Sunday Nation* for upwards of two years. And that was what I continued to do in Dar-es-Salaam....
>
> Working for the president, between September 1970 and January 1973, was probably the most enjoyable period of my entire journalistic career. There were at least two reasons for this.
>
> The first was that ours was a community of ideas. The second, contrary to what was constantly claimed here in Nairobi and by the Western press, was that the Dar-es-Salaam newspapers enjoyed a high level of freedom to publish. This reflected the fact that Tanzania enjoyed an unprecedented freedom of speech. But it was never licentious freedom of the kind with which Nairobi's alternative press assails our eyes every morning.
>
> Following the Arusha Declaration of 1967, Julius Kambarage Nyerere had, early in 1970, nationalised *The Tanganyika Standard* from Lonhro and rechristened it *The Standard Tanzania* (sic) as the official print organ of the government. *The Nationalist* and its Kiswahili sister *Uhuru* already existed as the organs of the ruling Tanganyika African National Union (TANU), with Ben Mkapa as its editor.
>
> Brought in from London as Managing Editor of *The Standard* was a tough-talking South African woman of Asian origin called Frene Ginwala. Ginwala, who is now the Speaker of the South African Parliament in Cape Town, was a woman of strong left-wing convictions. She very soon collected around men and women from the international community with equally strong socialist views.
>
> This was the context in which I left Nairobi for Dar-es-Salaam, invited by Ginwala. Mwalimu Nyerere acted as our - non-executive - Editor-in-Chief. And yet every Friday I published an opinion column highly critical of his system.
>
> I waxed critical especially of the recent nationalised commercial and industrial houses: the corruption that was beginning to invade them and their umbrella organisations, the ineptitude, the apparent absence of development ideas. Yet never once did Ginwala or myself receive a telephone call from or a summons to Ikulu - State House - complaining about anything we had written. Of course, there were many murmurs in the corridors of power against us. They accused us of being a bunch of communists, though we never were. But they dared not call a press conference to attack us. Nyerere simply would not have allowed them to do so....

Kambarage Nyerere remained one of Africa's quintessential men of the 20th century. His personal probity was unequalled...(as was) his refusal to use his immense power to enrich himself or his family.

It was his intellectual strength and moral fiber that enabled him, when he saw that his (socialist) experiment could not succeed, to admit openly that his life career had been a failure.

When he nationalised *The Tanganyika Standard*, he gave us a charter, which expressly challenged its news editors to criticise all social failings by whomever they are committed. I had never been and would never be freer than when I worked in Dar....

This freedom of the press...was only a mirror-reflection of the much more important freedom of ideas throughout the country. Though Nyerere believed more than 100 per cent in Ujamaa, he never tried to force it down anybody's throat. Nor did he ever issue *The Standard*, *The Nationalist* or the latter's Swahili daily and weekly counterparts *Uhuru* and *Mzalendo*, with any instruction to print only Nyereist ideas or to slant news in favour of that ideology and its exponents.

If that had been the case, Tanzania's amazing pluralism of ideas at that time would not have reached the world. Yet it did reach the world, attracting into that country hundreds of intellectuals from all over the world. The University of Dar-es-Salaam at Ubungo was Africa's, perhaps the world's, intellectual Mecca.

Dar-es-Salaam harboured all the radical liberation movements in Africa, Latin America, the Middle East, Ireland, South-East Asia, even the United States. It was a crossroads of such celebrated freedom fighters as Agostinho Neto, Samora Machel, Marcelino dos Santos, Jorge Rebello, Janet Mondlane, Yoweri Museveni, Sam Nujoma, Thabo Mbeki, Oliver Tambo, Gora Ebrahim, Amilcar Cabral, Angela Davis and others, changing ideas with us, often hotly....

There were intellectuals - both native and alien - who expressed ideas so far to the right that they bordered on fascism. Others expressed ideas so far to the left that again they bordered on fascism.... For these were not uniform minds.... The humdinger, however, was that all these ideas were expressed freely and printed in the party and government newspapers with little attempt at editorial slanting and chicanery....

Until his death, Nyerere, who was humble, self-effacing and selfless, continued to serve humanity on many capacities - particularly his promotion of mutual South-South assistance to reduce dependence on Western alms and his attempt to bring about order in Burundi.

An intellectual of immense stature, a man of great personal integrity, a paragon of humanism, Julius Kambarage Nyerere will be hard to replace in Tanzania, in Africa and on the globe. I was privileged to know and work with such a man. That is why, as I mourn, I ask, with Marcus Antonius, whence cometh such another?[15]

Members of the entire editorial staff were fully aware of the kind of freedom we had to criticize the government, although we worked for a government-owned newspaper. But the government owned it on behalf of the people, *wananchi*. Therefore we were free to criticize leaders and policies and express our views across the spectrum without being censured. President Nyerere established that as a policy.

Our editors, first Sammy Mdee who later became President Nyerere's press secretary, and next Ben Mkapa who was elected president of Tanzania in 1995 and won a second five year-term in 2000, did not violate this policy which was adopted after the newspaper was nationalized. They sometimes even invited reporters to write or contribute to editorials. Self-criticism was also routine. Every morning before we went out on assignments, we had a post-mortem of the paper presided over by the editor, dissecting the stories we wrote the previous day.

Such was the camaraderie, the ambiance and egalitarian disposition, and freedom, we enjoyed at our newspaper; the largest English daily in Tanzania and one of the three largest and most influential in East Africa as a whole.

Although we were independent and wrote whatever we wanted to write, we were also at the center of a maelstrom because of the ideological ferment that the country was undergoing during that period in its quest for socialist transformation in pursuit of the egalitarian ideals of *Ujamaa* (which means familyhood in Kiswahili) espoused by Nyerere: a political theorist and philosopher, scholar and politician, without an equal on the continent in terms of intellectual depth and prowess and pursuits among leaders with the exception of President Leopold Sedar Senghor of Senegal, a poet-philosopher - "I feel, therefore I am," he mused, reminiscent of Rene Descartes, "I think, therefore I am"; and Dr. Kwame Nkrumah, president of Ghana and revolutionary thinker and theoretician.

But Nkrumah was overthrown in February 1966 in a CIA-engineered coup before Nyerere enunciated his socialist ideology in the Arusha Declaration almost exactly one year later in February 1967 after the Ghana coup.

So, with Nkrumah gone - he died in April 1972, six years after he was overthrown - only Nyerere and Senghor remained on the scene as the leading political thinkers among leaders on the continent.

I remember when Nkrumah died. I was at work on that day at the *Daily News* when the bulletin about his death came in on the telex in the evening in our editorial office. One of the first persons to express profound shock was Karim Essack, about whom more later, but Dr. Nkrumah's death equally affected the rest of us who read the news bulletin that evening. The other reporters were gone by then.

Although Nkrumah's death left on the scene two towering intellectual presidents, Nyerere and Senghor, it was Nyerere who, between the two, was far more influential on the continent and in the international arena.

Senghor was also seen as a white man in a black skin. But his unabashed Francophilia did not diminish his stature as an intellectual, especially among his admirers, and even among some of his critics who saw him as a black Frenchman who should have been born white and brought up in France. In 1980, he stepped down as president of Senegal and went to live in France where he died in December 2001 at the age of 95.

He was one African leader - and there were many others - who was not admired by many reporters on our editorial staff, anymore than Dr. Hastings Kamuzu Banda, the president of Malawi, was. I didn't know any on our staff who admired Banda.

Our newspaper, like the country itself, attracted not only reporters and revolutionary thinkers from different parts of Africa and beyond but also reporters of different ideological interests within Tanzania itself. There was, for instance, Karim Essack - a Tanzanian of Asian (Indian) origin - who was a leftist revolutionary and, like the rest of us on our editorial staff who were not leftist although some were, also an uncompromising foe of apartheid and other oppressive regimes.

He also wrote a book about Dr. Eduardo Mondlane and the liberation struggle in Mozambique and maintained, until his death in 1997, close ties with revolutionaries and radical thinkers around the world including many in Latin America. As the socialist-oriented International Emergency Committee (IEC) - founded to defend the life of Dr. Abimael Guzman, a Peruvian Marxist philosophy professor and leader of the revolutionary group Shining Path, captured and imprisoned in Peru in 1992 -

stated in October 1997 in its eulogy, "In Memory of Karim Essack":

> The IEC coordinating committee was saddened to learn that Karim Essack died this summer. He was a Tanzanian anti-imperialist who, for several decades, actively supported national liberation movements across the world. Karim Essack was a friend of the Peruvian people and a supporter of the People's War in Peru who dedicated some of his writings to Dr. Guzman and other PCP fighters. He was a signatory to the IEC Call and helped propagate the campaign in Africa. He will be missed.[16]

Karim Essack was just one of the reporters of Asian descent on our staff, which was fully integrated: black African being in the majority; Asian, mostly of Indian and Pakistani origin; Arab; and British. This also reflected Nyerere's ideals. As Tanzania's president and editor-in-chief of our newspaper, he would not have tolerated an editorial team that was exclusivist and intentionally did not reflect the racial and ethnic composition of our society - although, for practical purposes, not every "tribe" or ethnic group could have been represented on our staff or any anywhere else in the country.

But the bedrock principle on which our society was built under Nyerere was that no one should be discriminated against. And he meant what he said. Few countries in the world can match Tanzania's record of inclusion. And it is not uncommon to hear people from other countries who have lived in Tanzania say, "There is no racism and tribalism in Tanzania"; "Tanzania is the only country in Africa that has conquered tribalism," as Keith Richburg says in his book *Out of America: A Black Man Confronts Africa*;[17] "There is very little tribalism - and racism - in Tanzania"; "Tribalism and racism are not major problems in Tanzania." The last statement is closest to reality.

And in keeping with Tanzania's policy of welcoming refugees and promoting Pan-African solidarity as enunciated by Nyerere, members of our editorial staff from other African countries were not only guaranteed equal rights and accorded full protection like the rest of us, but also career advancement like everywhere else in Tanzania. So were other non-citizens from outside Africa.

In fact, in the 1970 general elections, people from other African countries who were not citizens of Tanzania were allowed to vote. President Nyerere allowed that as one of the ways of promoting African unity. And it is possible some of them even voted against him. But his gesture of goodwill was highly appreciated and resonated far beyond our national borders.

At our newspaper, some of the foreign reporters who held responsible positions included Tommy Sithole, sports editor, who returned to Zimbabwe and became managing editor of the state-owned *Zimbabwe Herald* after his country won independence under the leadership of Robert Mugabe, himself of scholarly bent like Nyerere, although not of the same intellectual stature and influence as a Pan-African leader. Sithole later became the only highest-ranked African on the International Olympic Committee (IOC) as IOC director of international cooperation and development.

There was also Philip Ochieng', a Kenyan, who wrote a weekly column, "The Way I See It." He also served as a sub-editor, one among several, including Felix Kaiza, Pascal Shija, Robert Rweyemamu, Uli Mwambulukutu, Abdallah Ngororo, Kassim Mpenda, Jenerali Ulimwengu, Emmanuel Bulugu, and a few others.

The news editor was Nsubisi Mwakipunda. Two senior reporters, Reginald Mhango - originally from Malawi - who later in 2002 became managing editor of the *Guardian,* one of Tanzania's leading daily newspapers, and Kusai Khamisa, also served as acting news editors in Mwakipunda's absence. All these were Tanzanians.

Philip Ochieng' eventually went back to Kenya - after further studies in Germany - and served as editor of the government-owned *Kenya Times* before returning to the *Daily Nation*, Nairobi, where he worked before he joined our editorial staff at the *Standard*, later *Daily News*, in Dar es Salaam. He also wrote a book, *I Accuse the Press: An Insider's View of the Media and Politics in Africa.*[18]

We also had sub-editors from South Africa, Nigeria, and Britain. The Nigerian sub-editor came from Biafra and fled his country during the civil war and was one of the many Eastern Nigerians, mostly Igbos, who sought asylum in Tanzania after the Eastern Region seceded from the Nigerian Federation. They included judges and professors, many other professionals and others who came to live in Tanzania during that critical period.

And many remained in Tanzania after the war. It was Nyerere who extended such hospitality to them after Tanzania became the first country to recognize Biafra. And in Dar es Salaam even today, there is a place called Biafra Grounds where mass rallies are held. There are also many Nigerians including professionals living in Tanzania.

They would not have been able to live and work in Tanzania in such large numbers had it not been for Tanzania's track record of hospitality initiated by Nyerere way back in the sixties soon after Tanganyika won independence from Britain on December 9, 1961. And as Dr. M.O. Ene, chairman of the Enyimba Pan-Igbo Think Tank, said about Nyerere when he died: "I saw the legend in 1966, and the memory still lives with me."

His Pan-African commitment and achievements were internationally acknowledged, despite his failed socialist policies. As Professor Harvey Glickman who made a study tour of Tanzania stated in his article, "Tanzania: From Disillusionment to Guarded Optimism," in *Current History: A Journal of Contemporary World Affairs*:

> Tanzania's profile, in the life and career of President Julius Nyerere, was poor, earnest, caring, and honest - at least until 1985, when Nyerere formally stepped aside in a peaceful constitutional transition (which is extremely rare in Africa). Tanzania's government was stable while other African governments succumbed to coups and civil wars.
>
> The country conducted consecutive national elections at regular five-year intervals. Other one-party states ignored mass participation; Nyerere's Tanzania devised a system of constituency primaries under the party umbrella, controlled at the center, but offering a voice for localism.
>
> Other African governments extolled the virtues of Pan-Africanism; Nyerere engineered the union of his own country and an offshore neighbor. Other African governments denounced white racist governments on the continent; Tanzania took action, cutting off relations with Britain over the issue of African rule in Rhodesia in 1965 (the first country to do so), and offering shelter to the liberation parties and guerrilla forces of southern Africa.
>
> While most African governments rejected the secession of Biafra from Nigeria in 1967, Tanzania recognized Biafra's short-lived government on moral grounds (and was the first to recognize the secessionist region), arguing it was an act of self-defence against ethnic pogroms. While other African countries merely denounced Idi Amin in Uganda in the 1970s, Tanzania's army defeated him in battle in 1979 and drove him from the country.[19]

And Nyerere's policy of good neighborliness and Pan-African solidarity was also clearly evident at our newspaper which had an exchange program with neighboring Zambia and whose president, Dr. Kenneth Kaunda, was Nyerere's ideological compatriot and very close personal friend. A reporter from the *Times of Zambia*, Francis Kasoma joined our editorial staff while our news editor Nsubisi Mwakipunda went to Zambia to work at the *Times*. Kasoma covered some of the most important political events in the country just as we did. It didn't matter he and a number of other reporters were not Tanzanians.

After working at the *Daily News* for quite some time, Kasoma returned to Zambia and years later became a professor and head of the mass communications department at the University of Zambia. He also wrote some books including *The Press and Multiparty Politics in Africa*.[20] He died in 2004.

Another member of our editorial staff who also wrote a book was deputy editor Hadji Konde. He also died and was one of the most renowned Tanzanian journalists with vast experience in the profession. He wrote *Press Freedom in Tanzania*.[21] His work was preceded only by Karim Essack's among those written by newsmen who worked at the *Daily News*, Dar es Salaam, Tanzania.

Another reporter on our editorial staff, Clement Ndulute, also became an author with the publication of his book, *The Poetry of Shaaban Robert*,[22] published in 1994 by the Dar es Salaam University Press. It is a translation of the works of Tanzania's eminent poet from Kiswahili into English. Ndulute went on to pursue further studies at the University of Indiana in the United States where he obtained his PhD in literature.

He returned to Tanzania and became a lecturer in literature at the University of Dar es Salaam, Tanzania. He then went back to the United States and became an associate professor of African literature at Mississippi Valley State University. He was at this writing a professor of English at Tuskegee University in Alabama.

Another member of our editorial staff who became a professor is Issa Kaboko Musoke. He attended Michigan State University in the United States during the seventies when I was also a student in the same state. He returned to Tanzania and joined the academic staff at the University of Dar es Salaam teaching sociology. He also taught in Botswana for some time.

Yet another reporter from the *Daily News* who also attended school in Michigan around the same time I did, was Deogratias Michael Masakilija. Both of us were sponsored by the Pan-African Congress-USA, an organization based in Detroit and founded by a group of African Americans in that city to strengthen ties between Black America and Africa and promote African unity.

Their Pan-African philosophy was based on the teachings of Kwame Nkrumah and Julius Nyerere who were the ideological mentors of the organization. They even had the pictures of the two leaders on the wall in their conference hall, together with those of Ahmed Sekou Toure, Malcolm X and Patrice Lumumba. These were the five leaders they admired the most and whose writings they studied for ideological guidance and inspiration.

Tanzania's national dress, the dark suit with a collar-less jacket worn by President Nyerere and other Tanzanian leaders, was the official attire of the male members of the organization. Many Pan-African Congress members also took lessons in Kiswahili which they regarded as a Pan-African language. Some of the members of the organization went to live or work in Tanzania, while others simply visited the country, one of their favorites, together with Ghana.

And a number of others attended the Sixth Pan-African Congress under the stewardship of President Julius Nyerere held at the University of Dar es Salaam in Nkrumah Hall in 1974. It was the first one held on African soil.

The last one, the Fifth Pan-African Congress, was held in Manchester, England, in 1945, and was attended by a number of future African leaders including Kwame Nkrumah, Jomo Kenyatta, Nnamdi Azikiwe, and Dr. Hastings Kamuzu Banda. It galvanized the African independence movement.

Dr. Banda's residence in London became a meeting place for African nationalists including Nkrumah whom Dr. Banda cordially called, "My boy." Nkrumah and others called Banda "the Doc."

After Ghana won independence and Nkrumah became president, Banda went to live and work in Ghana before returning to Nyasaland.

Other students who were sponsored or supported by the Pan-African Congress-USA and attended Wayne State University in Detroit during the same time I did were Kojo Yankah from Ghana who became a member of parliament and cabinet member under President Jerry Rawlings in the 1990s; as well as Amadou Taal and Mamadou Sohna, both from the Gambia.

When Amadou Taal returned to the Gambia, he became a high government official and the country's leading economist appointed by President Dawda Jawara, Gambia's first president. He held the following posts consecutively: Principal Planner in the Ministry of Economic Planning and Industrial Development; Permanent Secretary in the Ministry of Agriculture, and Permanent Secretary in the Ministry of Local Government and Lands.

Coincidentally, one of his closest friends, Hassan Jallow who got his law degree from the University of Dar es Salaam in Tanzania in the early seventies, became Gambia's attorney-general and later minister of justice under President Jawara. In 2003, Jallow was appointed by UN Secretary-General Kofi Annan and by the Security Council as the UN chief prosecutor of the International Criminal Tribunal for Rwanda (ICTR) based in Arusha, Tanzania.

And throughout his tenure, Amadou Taal represented the Gambia at international conferences in many countries including Tanzania. He served until Jawara was overthrown in a military coup in July 1994.

He was not sponsored by the Pan-African Congress-USA but was supported by the organization, as was Mamadou Sohna who later became a professor at a university in Virginia in the United States.

Another student who was sponsored by the Pan-African Congress-USA but did not attend Wayne State University and entered public life when he returned home was Kwabena Dompre from Ghana. He was the third student to be sponsored by the organization after Kojo Yankah; and Olu Williams from Sierra Leone who attended the University of Nebraska and obtained a doctorate in agricultural economics. He died in 2000 in Sierra Leone.

Kwabena went to Western Michigan University. After he returned to Ghana, he entered politics and worked as a high ranking official for President Hilla Limann. He later studied law in Ghana and in the United States.

We all lived in the same house owned by the Pan-African Congress-USA which was also a meeting place for Pan-African Congress members, a number of African students and others including members of the Republic of New Afrika, engaged in lively conversations about the liberation struggle in southern Africa, African politics in general, the civil rights struggle in the United States and other subjects. It was an environment highly conducive to cross-fertilization of ideas across the spectrum, and it left a lasting impression on me and others.

My other schoolmates at Wayne State University who went into public life, but who were not sponsored by the Pan-African Congress-USA, included Raphael Munavu who became a professor of chemistry at Nairobi University and then vice-chancellor of Moi University after he returned to Kenya. He obtained his PhD in chemistry from Wayne State University. Although an academic, his position as vice-chancellor of one of Kenya's universities made him a leading educational authority and a public figure.

Another graduate of Wayne State University who was in a similar position but who went to school there long before I did was Dr. Philemon Msuya from Tanzania, assistant dean of Muhimbili Medical School in Dar es salaam headed by Dr. Nhonoli when I was a reporter at the *Daily News*. I once interviewed him and wrote a feature article about our country's medical school in our newspaper; that's how I learned that he was a graduate of Wayne State University Medical School, the largest in the United States.

My interview with Dr. Msuya had to do with high-level manpower and how we would meet our country's needs in the medical field. The projections by the Tanzanian government that we would have enough doctors by 1985 did not correspond to reality; a point I underscored in my article.

Wayne State University also had ties to Tanzania in other ways. Tanzania's junior minister of health and - together with Bibi Titi Mohammed - one of the first two female cabinet members in Tanganyika soon after independence, Lucy Lameck, also attended Wayne State University. And there were two professors from Tanzania, Mark Kiluma and Mayowera, who taught Kiswahili at Wayne State University when I was a student there in the seventies. And the head of the linguistics department at Wayne State University, Professor Sorensen, lived in Tanzania - what was then Tanganyika - for 25 years, and first went there before I was born. He was, all those years, a Catholic priest in Morogoro where I also lived when I was under five years old.

Besides the two Tanzanians teaching Kiswahili, other African professors at Wayne State University included Mxolisi Ntlabati from South Africa. An associate of Nelson Mandela and others who ended up in the dock in the Rivonia Trial, he would have been one of them had he not fled the country via Tanganyika and gone to the United States for further studies.

Tragically, he was killed in 1979 by the same apartheid regime he fled from, after he left Detroit, Michigan, and returned to South Africa and was banished to a remote part of Ciskei, one of the homelands, where the only job he could find was teaching at a secondary school and which severely limited his career opportunities in a deliberate effort by the white racist government to destroy him. He died at the hands of the authorities.

A strong admirer of President Julius Nyerere and his policies, he named one of his children Ujamaa in honor of Mwalimu Nyerere for his Pan-African solidarity and commitment to the liberation struggle. Dr. Ntlabati also served as pastor of the People's Community Church, one of the largest black churches in Detroit which was only a few yards away from the Pan-African Congress house where we lived. The church also sponsored one student from Ghana who lived in the church building, with all his tuition and living expenses paid by the church members.

Another fellow African student at Wayne State University, Emmanuel Sendezera from Malawi, also ended up in South Africa as a physics professor at Witwatersrand University and at the University of Zululand in Kwazulu/Natal Province. He and John Muhanji from Kenya were the only two black PhD students in physics at Wayne State University in the seventies. They were also among the few students from East Africa on campus besides me, a few Kenyans, Ethiopians, and one Ugandan nun. And like

Raphael Munavu, John Muhanji also returned to Kenya.

Wayne State University also had students from many other African countries. And our organization on campus, the Organization of African Students (OAS) of which I was president, had a monthly publication called *Ngurumo*, which was also the name of a Swahili newspaper in Tanzania.

The students, most of whom came from West Africa, chose the name because they were attracted by its literal meaning, Thunder. And probably just as many said they liked the name because it reminded them of Nkrumah, an embodiment of Pan-Africanism, which our organization also embraced as a unifying ideology.

My association with this publication was the last I would have as a journalist. After I left Wayne State University, my life veered in another direction in terms of academic pursuits and career advancement. Years later, I ended up writing books, mostly academic works.

While Musoke and I never returned to journalism after finishing our studies in Michigan, Masakilija did. After he returned to Tanzania, he not only continued to work as a journalist but went on to pursue other interests as well in the private sector.

And one of our colleagues on the editorial staff at the *Daily News*, Abdallah Ngororo, who joined the government and became permanent secretary - head of the ministry's civil service - at different ministries under President Benjamin Mkapa, our former editor, died in 2002. Another colleague ours at the *Daily News*, Stanley Kamana, died in 2005. He was still working as a journalist more than thirty years after we worked together on the same editorial staff and was one of the most seasoned journalists in the country when he died.

And I came up way down the road as an author with my first book published in 1999, 27 years after I left the *Daily News*. And unlike the works of my colleagues all of which dealt with the press, except Ndulute's about poetry, mine was about economics, entitled, *Economic Development in Africa*,[23] which also came to be used as a college textbook mainly for graduate (post-graduate) studies in colleges and universities in the United States, Canada, Britain, Australia, South Africa and other countries, as have a number of other books I have written including *The Modern*

*African State: Quest for Transformation,*24 and *Africa and the West.*25

Although they are mostly found in university libraries around the world, and in a number of public libraries, they are also intended for members of the general public. I never intended to write them exclusively for the academic community. And I have taken the same approach in writing this book.

In *Economic Development in Africa*, I do acknowledge that our socialist policies failed, as President Nyerere himself admitted when he stepped down in November 1985 as much as he did on other occasions in the following years. But I also do know that Nyerere's economic policies were *not* - total failure. We had significant achievements in a number of areas. As I state on Amazon.com in my review of a book by George Ayittey, A Ghanaian professor of economics at The American University, *Africa in Chaos*:

> Ayittey has written an excellent book. In fact, I'm just as critical of Africa's despotic and kleptocratic regimes in all the books I have written. But I don't entirely agree with his assessment of Kwame Nkrumah, Julius Nyerere, and Kenneth Kaunda.
>
> He says his focus is not on the leadership qualities of any of the African leaders but on their policies. It is true that socialism failed to fuel economic growth. But an objective evaluation of what Nkrumah, Nyerere, and Kaunda did, shows that they had some success in a number of areas. Yet, Ayittey has almost nothing good to say about them in his book, *Africa in Chaos*. In fact, these are the three leaders of whom he's most critical in his book, devoting several pages to them more than any other African leader.
>
> Under Nkrumah, Ghana had the highest per capita income in sub-Saharan Africa. It was Nkrumah who laid the foundation for modern-day Ghana. He built the infrastructure that has sustained and fuelled Ghana's economic development through the years. It is true that there were also many failures under Nkrumah, and after he was gone; for example, institutional decay and crumbling infrastructure. But who built those institutions and the infrastructure?
>
> Nkrumah built schools, hospitals, roads, factories, dams and bridges, railways and harbours. Tens of thousands of people in Ghana who are lawyers, doctors, engineers, nurses, teachers, accountants, agriculturalists, scientists and others wouldn't be what they are today had it not been for the educational opportunities provided by Nkrumah.
>
> Ayittey talks about quality, saying that what mattered during Nkrumah's reign was quantity, not quality. What's the quality of the Ghanaian elite, including Ayittey himself, educated under Nkrumah? Are they not as good as anybody else? What was the quality of education at the University of Ghana,

Legon? Did it admit and train students of mediocre mental caliber? Did it have inferior academic programs? And an inferior faculty? Were more people dying in Ghanaian hospitals than they were being saved? Did the schools, hospitals, factories, roads and other infrastructure Nkrumah built do more harm than good? Would Ghana have been better off without them like Zaire under Mobutu?

In Tanzania, Nyerere also built schools, hospitals, clinics, factories, roads and railways, dams and bridges, hydroelectric power plants and other infrastructure. Although his policy of Ujamaa (meaning familyhood in Kiswahili) was not very successful, it did enable the country to bring the people together and closer to each other in order to provide them with vital social services.

The people had easier access to schools, clinics, clean water and other services provided by the government, than they otherwise would have been, because they lived closer to each other; which would have been impossible had they been spread too thin across the country, living miles and miles apart.

Also under Nyerere, education was free, from primary school all the way to the university level. Medical services were also free, in spite of the fact that Tanzania is one of the poorest countries in the world. Still, under Nyerere, it was able to afford all that. Everybody had equal opportunity.

Under his leadership, Tanzania also made quantum leaps in education. It had the highest literacy rate in Africa, and one of the highest in the world, higher than India's, which has one of the largest numbers of educated people and the third largest number of scientists after the United States and the former Soviet Union.

One of the biggest achievements under Nyerere was in the area of adult education. Tanzania, on a scale unprecedented anywhere else in the world, launched a massive adult education campaign to teach millions of people how to read and write. Within only a few years, almost the entire adult population of Tanzania - rural peasants, urban workers and others - became literate.

Almost everybody in Tanzania, besides children not yet in school, was able to read and write. And the University of Dar es Salaam in Tanzania became one of the most renowned academic institutions in the world, in less than ten years, with an outstanding faculty including some of the best and internationally acclaimed scholars from many countries.

Provision of vital services even to some of the most remote parts of the country - far removed from urban and social centers - was not uncommon although the services were, I must admit, curtailed through the years because of economic problems. Yet, all that was achieved under Nyerere who sincerely believed, and made sure, that everybody had equal access to the nation's resources. I know all this because I am a Tanzanian myself, born and brought up in Tanzania, and was one of the beneficiaries of Nyerere's egalitarian policies.

Tanzania has come a long way, and still has a long way to go. But give credit where credit is due, in spite of failures in a number of areas, and which must be acknowledged by all of us. I even admit that in my books.

But also look at where we were before: At independence in 1961,

Tanganyika (before uniting with Zanzibar in 1964 to form Tanzania) had only 120 university graduates, including two lawyers who had to draft and negotiate more than 150 international treaties for the young nation and handle other legal matters for the country. With 120 university graduates, Tanganyika was, of course, better off than the former Belgian Congo which had only 16 at independence in 1960, and Nyasaland (now Malawi) with only 34 at independence in 1964. Still, that was nowhere close to what Tanganyika would have been had the British tried to develop the colony; which was never their intention.

None of the 120 university graduates got their degrees in Tanganyika. There was no university in the country. The British never built one, and never intended to build one. Tanganyika built one after independence, and it became internationally renowned as an excellent academic institution in less than a decade.

The 120 university graduates Tanganyika had at independence was nothing in terms of manpower for a country; not even for a province or region. As Julius Nyerere said not long before he died:

'We took over a country with 85 percent of its adults illiterate. The British ruled us for 43 years. When they left, there were two trained engineers and 12 doctors. When I stepped down there was 91 percent literacy and nearly every child was in school. We trained thousands of engineers, doctors, and teachers.'

Nyerere stepped down in 1985. And all that was achieved within 24 years since independence. No mean achievement.[26]

The cornerstone of his economic policy for Tanzania's development was Ujamaa. And it was supported by the majority of Tanzanians, even if grudgingly by a significant number of them. But even some of the skeptics wanted to give it a chance. And when it failed, even Nyerere's harshest critics admitted that he meant well; which explains his enormous popularity across the country even after he stepped down, although the economy virtually came to a grinding halt especially during the last several years of his presidency.

He remained as popular as he was through the decades since independence and was even admired by some of his most ardent critics. As Jonathan Power, who once worked in Iringa, Tanzania, in the sixties as an agricultural officer (later as a journalist in Britain) and who was highly critical of Nyerere's policies and one party-rule, stated in his article, "Lament for Independent Africa's Greatest Leader":

Tanzania in East Africa has long been one of the 25 poorest countries in the world. But there was a time when it was described, in terms of its political influence, as one of the top 25. It punched far above its weight. That formidable achievement was the work of one man, now lying close to death in a London Hospital....

His extraordinary intelligence, verbal and literary originality... and apparent commitment to non-violence made him not just an icon in his own country but of a large part of the activist sixties' generation in the white world who, not all persuaded of the heroic virtues of Fidel Castro and Che Guevara, desperately looked for a more sympatheitc role model.

Measured against most of his peers, Jomo Kenyatta of Kenya, Kwame Nkrumah of Ghana, Ahmed Sekou Toure of Guinea, he towered above them. On the intellectual plane only the rather remote president of Senegal, the great poet and author of Negritude, Leopold Senghor, came close to him.

Not only was Nyerere financially open, modest and honest, he was uncorrupted by fame or position. He remained throughout his life, self-effacing and unpretentious. Above all, he inspired his own people to resist the tugs of tribalism and to pull together as one people. To this day Tanzania remains one of the very few African countries that has not experienced serious tribal division. Its continuously fraught relationship with the Arab-dominated off-shore island of Zanzibar is another matter.

Later, discarding his earlier more pacifist convictions, he was to become the eminence rise of the southern African liberation movements in Angola, Zimbabwe, Namibia and South Africa extending a wide open embrace to their operations. For this his country paid a heavy price, in material terms, but also because Nyerere's role as interlocutor with the West demanded enormous amounts of time and energy that often led him to neglect his domestic responsibilities....

Nyerere was not an egomaniac who banged the table and surrounded himself only with sycophants. He was simply the self-assured headmaster that he had been since his teaching days....

Tanzania remains one of the very poorest countries in the world.... Whereas a once equally poor nearby country, Botswana, has progressed rapidly to the point where it is barely recognizable as the impoverished backwater it was only thirty years ago, Tanzania remains mired in the rut of underdevelopment and only recently, since Nyerere voluntarily retired in 1985, has begun to make up for lost time.

For most of Nyerere's long period in office his country was in economic difficulties. Inherited poverty, appalling weather, world recessions, crazed neighbours and war in southern Africa were all parts of the problem, but in the end there was not a good excuse for such continuous failures....

Nyerere's Christian socialist ideology dreamed of new ways of organizing society when there were hardly the rudiments of modern structures.... His biggest mistake of all was what he called 'ujamaa' - a kind of African, Israeli kibbutz-inspired collectivisation....

Later Nyerere was to admit that even in his home village (Butiama), which he often liked to visit, ujamaa had not really taken hold. In the end he was forced to put ujamaa on a back burner, but the damage had been done.

Many of us will mourn Julius Nyerere when he is gone. He was, without any doubt, second only to Nelson Mandela, the most inspiring African leader of his generation.[27]

Although most Tanzanians - and millions of other Africans - were indeed inspired by Nyerere, there were many who disagreed with him and did not like his policies, especially socialism and one-party rule. And like the general population, our editorial staff at the *Daily News* was not a monolithic whole. Many reporters professed to be socialist or supported Tanzania's socialist policies. But some were clearly at the other end of the ideological spectrum, including a number of those who claimed to be socialist and strong supporters of Nyerere's ujamaa policies.

This dichotomy or ambivalence is probably best explained by Nyerere's sincerity and enormous popularity among the masses. Reporters were part of the elite. So, going against the president who was the embodiment of the wishes and aspirations of the poor peasants and workers, and who articulated their sentiments, would have been "treacherous" and "unpatriotic," some of them felt; in spite of the fact that he encouraged us to be critical and freely express our views.

Yet few people - anywhere across the country - wanted to be seen as uncaring, betraying the masses. Therefore for some on our editorial staff, it was self-censorship, to identify themselves with the poor peasants and workers who constituted the vast majority of the population and the backbone of our economy. They were the nation. Many people including reporters found it hard to criticize Nyerere.

His sincerity, humility, and deep concern for the masses confounded even some of his most persistent critics, as did his disarming and startling candor. And even after he stepped down from the presidency, he did not hesitate to criticize his successor whenever he felt such criticism was warranted. And he was blunt about it, and applauded for his honesty and deep concern for the well-being of the nation. Even newsmen, known for their distrust of politicians, applauded him:

> Former Tanzanian president Julius Nyerere on Tuesday (March 13, 1995) accused the government of President Ali Hassan Mwinyi of corruption and

violating the constitution and urged Tanzanians to vote differently in the next elections.

Addressing a gathering of local and foreign journalists at the Kilimanjaro International Hotel here (in Dar es Salaam), Nyerere also accused Mwinyi's administration of condoning religious differences and tribalism.

'This would not only lead to the collapse of the now-sensitive 30-year-old union between the twin-islands of Zanzibar and Pemba and Tanzania mainland, but would also plunge the country into chaos,' Nyerere warned and urged Tanzanians to ensure that they voted for 'a president able to correct the situation and put the country on the right track.'

Nyerere, who ruled Tanzania for 24 years after independence from British colonial rule in 1961, described Tanzania as a country 'stinking with corruption.'

'Corruption in Tanzania has no bounds. Every country I visit they talk about corruption in Tanzania. Tanzania is stinking with corruption,' Nyerere told journalists gathered at the Tanzania Press Club.

Referring to a tax fraud in the country that recently led to aid suspension by donor countries and organisations, Nyerere declared: 'This was one quality of corruption. Any government that works for the wealthy does not collect tax, it chooses to harass small-time dealers,' Nyerere charged.

Nyerere, affectionately referred to as 'Mwalimu (Teacher) and Father of the Nation' by Tanzanians, said he was speaking of qualities required of a future president to avoid plunging the country into total collapse.

Comparing Tanzania to 'a house that has just been completed,' Nyerere said 'the country has been hit by a tremor, developing cracks which must be filled,' and said the cracks were 'the political union between Zanzibar and the mainland, corruption, religious tensions, tribalism, the constitutional crisis and lack of rule of law.'

In an apparent reference to President Mwinyi himself, Nyerere told the journalists that Tanzania needed a leader who will defend and promote the national constitution. 'It can't be a person that gets advice from his wife, and tomorrow we see some decision has been made. You can't have such a guy. You won't know what his wife will advise him,' Nyerere said amid applause from more than 100 journalists attending the gathering.

Tanzania goes to the polls next October (1995) in the first multi-party presidential and parliamentary elections since the country attained independence 34 years ago.[28]

Much as Nyerere was revered, he remained humble until his last days. His humility and genuine compassion for the masses was probably the most prominent quality of his long political career spanning almost half a century.

I particularly remember one incident in 1972 when another reporter, Stanley Kamana, and I were assigned to cover the president. More than 30 years later, Kamana was still a journalist and one of the leading veterans in the profession in the country, together with my other former colleagues at the *Daily News*, including Kassim Mpenda who became director of Radio Tanzania, Dar es Salaam (RTD), and later Tanzania's director of information services at the ministry of information and broadcasting, as he still was at this writing.

So was Charles Kizigha who was still at the *Daily News*, an enduring phenomenon at the paper for three decades after I left the editorial staff; Reginald Mhango, a senior reporter for 30 years who was appointed editor of the *Guardian*, Tanzania, in 2002; Jenerali Ulimwengu, one of the two lawyers who were reporters on our editorial staff, who became chairman and publisher, Habari Corporation, responsible for the publication of several newspapers in Kiswahili; Pascal Shija who became managing editor of *The Express*; and our former editor Sammy Mdee who was appointed chairman of the Tanzania Broadcasting Services (TBS) by President Mkapa in 2003.

When my colleagues and I were together at the *Daily News* 30 years ago, covering the president with Stanley Kamana on that day was one of the main assignments I was given, besides covering parliament which I did many times, only a few months before I left for the United States to pursue further studies.

President Nyerere addressed a mass rally in Dar es Salaam where he criticized the authorities of the Coast Region (Mkoa wa Pwani, in Kiswahili) for ordering the demolition of stands owned by hawkers on a major street, Ilala, which feeds into Pugu Road that goes all the way to the national airport.

Foreign dignitaries from a number of countries were coming to Dar es Salaam in only a few days to attend a major conference. But the regional officials, including Regional Commissioner Mustafa Songambele who was also at the rally, did not want these dignitaries to see the peddlers and their stands on this major route they were going to take on their way into the city from the airport. They felt ashamed and did not want to "humiliate" and "embarrass" our country.

The hawkers and their stands were, in fact, more than any eyesore, according to these officials. Such a spectacle could not be reconciled with our determination to maintain national dignity in spite of all the poverty we had and still have in Tanzania. That was the twisted logic of these leaders.

In his public address, President Nyerere asked about the peddlers: "What have they done wrong? What do you want them to do without income? What are you going to give them instead, once you demolish the stands? That's the only means they have to earn a living." Some stands had already been demolished, but the rest were not, after Nyerere's speech.

What happened then reminds me of what happened in 1998 when American President Bill Clinton visited Ghana and other African countries. Many government officials in Accra, Ghana's capital, did not want Clinton and his entourage to see the open sewage in the capital. President Jerry Rawlings ordered them to leave everything as it was so that the Americans should "see the way we live." Just covering it up won't solve the problem. Once the Americans are gone, the raw sewage will still be there.

Nyerere, for whom Rawlings had profound respect, had the same attitude. Impressing foreigners was not part of his personality. His biggest concern was the well-being of the poor, the downtrodden, the oppressed.

With or without the stands on Ilala Street, the visiting dignitaries would probably not even have noticed any difference, any way, and would not have been impressed either way. Nyerere's response to the callous indifference of the Coast Region government officials is an enduring memory I have always cherished. And it should be a lesson for other African leaders who claim that they care about their people while they are busy doing exactly the opposite.

Another memorable but tragic occasion during my career as a reporter in Tanzania was when I covered the country's first vice president, Sheikh Abeid Karume, who was also president of Zanzibar. Our constitution allowed that because Zanzibar was an autonomous - not a sovereign - entity within the union. And it still is, although there have been some changes stipulating that the country shall have only one vice president, not two as before (one from the isles and the other from the mainland), and that contenders for the presidency and vice presidency can come from anywhere in the union without any restrictions except those prescribed by law. The changes took place after multiparty democracy was introduced in the early 1990s.

I covered Karume in 1972 not long after I returned to Dar es Salaam from Zanzibar where I had been sent with another reporter, Juma Penza, to cover the eighth anniversary of the Zanzibar revolution of January 1964. A senior reporter at the *Daily News*, Penza later became deputy publicity secretary of Tanzania's ruling party (CCM) and still held that post in the 1990s and beyond.

We were in Zanzibar for several days. Karume came to Dar es Salaam after we got back from Zanzibar and gave a speech at the Police Officers' Mess in Msasani, an area on the outskirts of the capital where President Nyerere also lived in a simple house, away from his official residence, Ikulu (State House).

Speaking in Kiswahili, Karume told the officers to examine their inner selves in order to conduct themselves in an exemplary manner when performing their duties. That was his last speech in Dar es Salaam and on the mainland. He returned to Zanzibar and, not long afterwards, was assassinated on April 7 in a hail of bullets.

He was reportedly shot eight times at close range. Coincidentally or not, he had also been in office for eight years as first vice president of Tanzania. The number of times he was shot may have been deliberately calculated to symbolize the number of years he had been in office - one bullet for each year - if indeed he was hit eight times.

Abdulrahman Mohammed Babu, a Zanzibari from Pemba Island and senior cabinet member in the union government and one of the most prominent Tanzanian leaders, was accused by the Zanzibari authorities of masterminding the assassination and detained on the mainland in 1972 in connection with the murder. But President Nyerere refused to send him back to Zanzibar where he probably would have been executed, as Kassim Hanga was, under a judicial system that had little regard for justice and individual rights, let alone for those accused of killing the country's first vice president.

As an autonomous entity, Zanzibar also had its own judicial system whose dispensation of justice differed from what we had on the mainland in many fundamental respects.

After Babu was released from detention in 1978, he left Tanzania and went to Britain. He later became a professor of international relations at San Francisco State University, California, in the United States.

He died in Britain in 1996 and the Tanzanian government brought his body back home and assumed full responsibility for his funeral expenses in acknowledgment of his status as a national leader, regardless of whatever differences he may have had with his colleagues including President Nyerere himself.

Karume's assassination was the first of a Tanzanian leader since independence, preceded by Tom Mboya's in neighboring Kenya only three years before in July 1969.

Aboud Jumbe succeeded Karume and became Zanzibar's president and Tanzania's first vice president under Nyerere, but resigned in 1984 because of his dissatisfaction with the structure of the union.

Rashidi Kawawa, a veteran politician since independence who together with Nyerere and Oscar Kambona constituted a trio and the most influential political team in Tanzania until Kambona went into self-imposed exile in Britain in July 1967, was the country's second vice president. President Nyerere continued to lead Tanzania until November 1985 when he voluntarily stepped down after being in office for 24 years since independence from Britain on December 9, 1961. It was a long political career, marked by successes and failures.

A lot has been said about the failure of his economic policies. But little has been said about his achievements. As he told the World Bank in 1998: "We took over a country with 85 percent of its adults illiterate. The British ruled us for 43 years. When they left, there were two trained engineers and 12 doctors. When I stepped down there was 91 percent literacy and nearly every child was in school. We trained thousands of engineers, doctors and teachers."[29]

He was painfully aware of our long, tortuous journey since independence, being one of the few university graduates himself when he assumed stewardship of the nation. He was, in fact, the first African from Tanganyika to obtain a master's degree in 1952 at Edinburgh University in Scotland where he studied economics, history, and philosophy.

We had very few trained people and had to rely on expatriates in most fields. But because of his excellent leadership, we were able to achieve a lot in only a few years.

I, myself, would not be what I am today had it not been for his leadership. And you wouldn't be reading this book or any of the others I have written. And the reason is simple: I would not have been able to go to school.

Under his leadership, education was free for everybody, unlike today. Medical service was also free, again unlike today. Even transportation for us to go to boarding school, to any part of the country, was free, paid for by the government; which means by the peasants and workers of Tanzania, with their tax money. We all had equal opportunity to be the best we could be. Few countries can claim that, and mean it. Tanzania did that, because of Nyerere.

But none of this would have been possible had the country not been united. There was a strong possibility back in the sixties and even in the seventies that our country could have fallen apart or been plunged into chaos, fractured along tribal and regional and even religious lines, if we had poor leadership; especially under the multiparty system which capitalizes on greed and partisan interests as has happened in Tanzania since the introduction of multiparty politics, although it doesn't have to be that way if the parties involved transcend sectarianism and ethno-regional loyalties. As Nyerere said many years after his retirement:

> I really think that I ran the most successful single-party system on the continent. You might not even call it a party. It was a single, huge nationalist movement....
>
> I don't believe that our country would be where it is now if we had a multiplicity of parties, which would have become tribal and caused us a lot of problems.
>
> But when you govern for such a long time, unless you are gods, you become corrupt and bureaucratic.... So I started calling for a multiparty system.[30]

Neighboring Kenya faced the same problem, regional fragmentation, when one of the political parties, the Kenya African Democratic Union (KADU) led by Ronald Ngala - a former teacher and prominent politician in the Coast Province - pursued a regionalist agenda which could have split the country along ethno-regional lines. Or it could have weakened the central government so much that national leaders would not have been able to exercise any power over the regions.

His agenda was also supported by many other Kenyans who were not members of KADU, especially those from smaller tribes. And there is still strong interest in *majimboism* (regionalism) even today in Kenya, mainly because of the political dominance of the ruling party, the Kenya African National Union (KANU), which seemed to be destined to rule perpetually until it was defeated in the 2002 general election by a coalition of opposition parties, NARC, ending almost 40 years of hegemonic control of Kenya. *Majimbo*, a Kiswahili word, means provinces or regions; *jimbo* being its singular form.

But Jomo Kenyatta succeeded in establishing a unitary state under a strong central government to keep the country united like Nyerere did in Tanganyika, later Tanzania. The difference is that Kenya's ruling party, KANU, was dominated by the Kikuyu, Kenyatta's tribe and the country's biggest; while in Tanganyika, the ruling Tanganyika African National Union (TANU) was pluralistic. No single tribe became dominant; another great achievement by Nyerere.

Yet, Ngala's quest for regional autonomy in Kenya seems to have been vindicated by President Kenyatta himself because of his dictatorial instincts. He was highly sensitive to criticism and neutralized his opponents quickly. That is what he did to his vice president, Oginga Odinga, who resigned and went on to form the opposition party, the Kenya People's Union (KPU), based on egalitarian ideals like Nyerere's to pursue policies which would benefit the masses, not just the elite like KANU's under Kenyatta did. Odinga accused Kenyatta's government of ignoring and exploiting *wananchi*, the people, and was neutralized, with Kenyatta claiming, "I have been kind for too long."[31]

Ronald Ngala also had a taste of Kenyatta's bile in parliament one day in a very distasteful way. As Mundia Kamau stated in his article, "A Nation in Distress," in Kenya's *Mashada Daily*:

> Jomo Kenyatta was not a democrat at all. He was the exemplification and personification of the African 'Big Man,' a ruthless dictator. Jomo Kenyatta carried on where the British left off, continuing with the plunder of public resources, and theft of public land. He mastered the art of oppression the African way, by ruthlessly exploiting the ignorance, biases, and prejudices of most Africans, a trend that still sadly persists....
>
> An example of Kenyatta's ruthless intolerance comes out in Koigi wa

Wamwere's autobiography when he states how Kenyatta once drew his gun in parliament intending to shoot the late Ronald Ngala for criticising his government, and was only restrained by then Speaker, Humphrey Slade.

The myth that Kenyatta was a democrat and professional must be dispensed with immediately, if we truly hope to solve the problems of this country. The only essential difference between Kenyatta and his successor Moi, is that Kenyatta was more widely travelled and more eloquent in English.[32]

Kenyatta may have been wrong in silencing Ronald Ngala and his opposition party, KADU, the way he did in parliament by threatening to shoot the opposition leader. Yet, the threat to national unity posed by extensive autonomy (*majimboism*, derived from majimbo) as advocated by Ngala and his party KADU, and by the multiparty system, cannot be ignored if such devolution of power is not implemented within prescribed limits and specifically designated areas of authority; and if multiparty democracy is allowed to thrive on ethno-regional loyalties and partisan interests at the expense of the nation. But this was not a major problem in Tanzania under Nyerere, although he decentralized power under a unitary state, something rarely done - if at all - in most highly centralized states across the continent.

Tragically, tribalism is beginning to gain a foothold in Tanzania, with tribal organizations emerging on the scene, tolerated or sanctioned by the state by invoking pluralism. And appeal to tribal and regional sentiments has become a feature of national politics since multiparty democracy was introduced in the early nineties.

The resurgence of this ugly phenomenon was underscored by former Vice President Joseph Sinde Warioba, also a distinguished jurist, in a speech in Dar es Salaam in March 2001. President Benjamin Mkapa himself was fully aware of these sectarian threats and won his second term with a promise to keep the country united, transcending ethinc, regional, racial and religious differences.

The re-introduction of multiparty politics, which has exacerbated the situation prompted many people to re-evaluate the transition from one-partyism to multipartyism. Many Tanzanians are probably having second thoughts about the wisdom of the decision by the national leaders who made this fundamental change against what was generally perceived to be popular will.

When the people across the country were asked in the early nineties whether or not Tanzania should adopt the multiparty system, it was reported that the majority of those who participated in the survey were opposed to the change.

That may be one of the reasons - besides poor organization, lack of direction, and personal rivalries - why opposition parties have not been able to win significant support in Tanzania; prompting one prominent opposition leader who rejoined the ruling party, CCM, in 2002 to say that CCM will rule Tanzania for the next 500 years. As the old saying goes, if you can't beat them, join them. A number of other opposition leaders and members have taken this pragmatic approach, which may also help to maintain national unity and stability.

Although I am in favor of multiparty democracy if it works well, I sometimes also have had strong reservations about the functional utility of the multiparty system in the African context because of its divisive tendencies and potential for catastrophe. To contend otherwise, given Africa's experience in many cases, is rank dishonesty or sheer naiveté. In most cases, the multiparty system tends to fuel tribal and regional rivalries.

But the one-party system itself is not above reproach when it discriminates against some groups and individuals as has been the case in most African countries - in Kenya under Kenyatta and Moi, favoring members of their tribes, the Kikuyu and the Kalenjin, respectively; Malawi under Banda whose government was dominated by the Chewa; Ivory Coast which was a *de facto* one-party state under Felix Houphouet-Boigny and Henri Bedie who favored members of their Baoule tribe, as did President Laurent Gbagbo, another Baoule; Togo under Gnassingbe Eyadema favoring members of his northern tribe, the Kabye, who also constituted 70 percent of the national army, to name only a few.

However, the multiparty system, more than the one-party system, can promote democracy in Africa if the people vote across tribal and regional lines to advance a common agenda. Yet, few African countries can honestly claim to have a majority of such voters who have transcended ethno-regional loyalties; a strong case for federalism and a limited number of parties as prescribed by law. Their interests are highly partisan. And they are not based on policy differences, bringing together members of different tribes and social and economic classes to pursue common interests. Their interests are defined by tribal and regional identities more than anything else.

The multiparty system is strongly advocated as a safeguard against corruption and dictatorship. It can, indeed, serve as a watchdog for the underdog to expose corruption, ensure transparency, and end dictatorship in African countries; but only if the parties don't, however surreptitiously, appeal to their regional constituencies to win elections. So, limit the number of political parties to broaden their base across the nation.

Have three parties at the most, or may be even two. And this will, in fact, strengthen the opposition because, more often than not, governments thrive on a divided opposition, making it easy for incumbents to win elections by fair means or foul. Therefore the opposition should be the first to support limiting the number of political parties, since this will help government opponents to mobilize forces into a cohesive bloc even if it is based on a coalition of interests, as is the case in politics in general. Politics is based on compromise.

But dominant political parties which are in power in African countries will probably be the last to support limiting the number of political parties, since this will help unite their opponents; unless a limited number of political parties is going to benefit them somehow, for example, by co-opting the opposition, thus reducing it to nothing.

The argument for a limited number of political parties is validated by experience. There are very few truly national parties in Africa. And if we can't form such parties which attract substantial numbers of people from all the tribes across the country as TANU - and even CCM - did under Nyerere and his successors, without lopsided membership, then only the one-party system can claim to be truly national; but only if it also embraces members of all tribes, is liberalized, and decentralized to curb autocratic instincts.

Under Nyerere, I remember when students openly questioned, without fear of retribution, the merits of the one-party system. For example, at Tambaza High School in Dar es Salaam, we had such free discussion - risky, and even deadly, in most African countries

- in class conducted by our headmaster, Mr. Lila (pronounced as Lee-la), a highly articulate man with profound insight into political theory and mass participatory politics.

He had thorough command of the subject and explained Nyerere's ideology well. And he supported it, yet was open to criticism; which was very encouraging and reassuring to the students. We were not muzzled.

We also knew the kind of opportunities we had. There were Asian (mostly Indian and Pakistani), Arab, and African students in my class. Yet, despite the fact that Tanzania was under a black majority government, the Asian and Arab students knew they had equal opportunity just like the rest of their fellow countrymen because of the kind of leadership and moral vision provided by Nyerere.

He led by example. Many students of different tribes and races went on to lead successful lives in different areas because of the equal opportunities provided by Nyerere. That was not the case in most African countries, including neighboring Kenya, where discrimination was rampant as it still is today.

In his cabinet since independence - and even before in 1960 when Tanganyika won self-government with Julius Nyerere as chief minister but still under colonial rule - he had members of all races, including women; for example, Derek Bryceson, an Englishman, who came to Tanganyika in 1951; Amir H. Jamal, an Indian; Abdulrahman Mohammed Babu, an Arab; Salim Ahmed Salim, also an Arab; Bibi Titi Mohammed, the first female cabinet member appointed as junior minister of community development soon after independence; Lucy Lameck, appointed as junior minister of health, also in the sixties and, together with Bibi Titi, one of Tanzania's most prominent leaders.

There was also Dr. Leader Stirling who was the oldest cabinet member and who outlived them all - those just mentioned including President Nyerere - and who was one of the first leaders of the independence movement in Tanganyika. Born in Britain in 1906, Dr. Stirling was a missionary doctor who came to Tanganyika in 1935.

He worked as a doctor in Masasi - home district of President Benjamin Mkapa - in southern Tanganyika for 24 years before entering politics. His political career began in 1958 when he became a member of the pre-independence parliament - known as LEGCO (Legislative Council) - as a representative of the Tanganyika African National Union (TANU), the party which led the country to independence. He served as minister of health from 1975 to 1980, and died in Dar es Salaam in February 2003 at the age of 96.

And these are only a few examples of the rainbow leadership of Tanzania, and a microcosm of what our country came to be, under President Nyerere.

There were many others - across the racial spectrum - in high government positions including the diplomatic service. In fact, Salim Ahmed Salim, former Tanzania's permanent representative to the United Nations, was recalled by Nyerere and given a succession of senior cabinet posts through the years. He once served as defence minister, minister of foreign affairs, and as prime minister.

He then went on to become secretary-general of the Organization of African Unity (OAU) in Addis Ababa, Ethiopia. He served for 12 years from 1989 to 2001; an unprecedented term, longer than any of his predecessors did, and was the last OAU secretary-general before the organization was transformed into the African Union (AU) at the last OAU meeting in June 2001 in Lusaka, Zambia.

But the actual transition was a gradual process, and the AU did not start functioning until later, after being formally launched in Durban, South Africa, in July 2002 under the chairmanship of South African President Thabo Mbeki.

When Salim Ahmed Salim was Tanzania's ambassador to the UN, he was almost elected UN secretary-general and won the support of the majority of the members in the General Assembly.

But the big powers had their own agendas and preferences and blocked his election. The United States did not want him at the helm because of Tanzania's relentless support of the People's Republic of China through the years to get the world's most populous nation admitted into the UN, instead of pretending that it did not exist, with Ambassador Salim being one of the strongest advocates even when he served in a neutral capacity as president of the UN General Assembly - he was still Tanzania's ambassador. And the Soviet Union did not want him because the

Russians felt that he was too independent and would not bend to their wishes. And it is possible he could even be elected president of Tanzania one day.

Following the death of Tanzania's Vice President Omar Ali Juma in July 2001, it was reported that Dr. Salim Ahmed Salim was the favorite of the political heavyweights in the country's ruling party, CCM, to succeed him but did not become vice president because he turned down the offer. Others claimed that because of his high international profile, he would have overshadowed President Benjamin Mkapa, and therefore turned down or was not given the post; although it is highly unlikely that Mkapa would have been eclipsed by Dr. Salim.

Mkapa is a man of such high intellectual caliber, strong personality and self-confidence, that it would have been virtually impossible to overshadow him; qualities which helped propel him to the highest position in the country as president with the full support of Nyerere. In fact, it was Nyerere who recommended him to be the presidential candidate of the ruling party, CCM, although he almost lost the nomination to Jakaya Mrisho Kikwete, a favorite among the younger members of the party, and won it by a small margin. In 2005, Kikwete was elected president of Tanzania. It was a landslide victory.

Whatever the case, Salim remained a formidable political personality and had a chance to be elected president in the future. But he was defeated by Kikwete who was nominated by the ruling party as its presidential candidate. Dr. Salim came in a distant second.

However, there is evidence everywhere across Tanzania showing that Nyerere built a truly pluralistic society with equal opportunity for all. My classmates are some of the beneficiaries, regardless of their tribal and racial identities. For example, one of them, Mohammed Chande Othman - he was simply called Chande - of Arab extraction, once served as a senior prosecution attorney and chief prosecutor at the International Criminal Tribunal for Rwanda (ICTR) established by the UN in Arusha, Tanzania.

He earned his law degree at the University of Dar es Salaam, one of the best law schools in Africa, and the first to be established in East Africa. After working at the UN court in Tanzania, he was assigned to East Timor where he was appointed general prosecutor - UN's chief prosecutor - to help the young southeast Asian nation establish its judicial system under UN auspices.

And there are countless other Tanzanians, of all races and tribes, who have reached the pinnacle of success through the years at home and abroad because of the foundation laid by Nyerere that has sustained Tanzania as a peaceful, stable country, with opportunities for all. And he did that with humility and simplicity which characterized his political career more than any other leader on the continent.

After Nyerere voluntarily stepped down as president of Tanzania in November 1985, it was with a simple bicycle that he returned to his home village of Butiama in northern Tanzania near the southeastern shores of Lake Victoria, to live and work on the farm; and eat simple breakfast of porridge with the children from poor families in the area. He did it every morning. As James Mpinga wrote in *The East African*:

> There is little to show that Butiama, the birthplace of Julius Nyerere, raised one of Africa's greatest sons. Mud huts surround the Catholic Church where Nyerere used to pray, and both the church and the mud huts tell a story. From the mud huts came the children who knew exactly when Mwalimu would have his breakfast, and dutifully came to share it with him every morning, and in the church their parents shared a common faith and prayer.
>
> 'At first it was bread and butter for both Mwalimu and the kids. Soon I couldn't cope with the increasing numbers of children joining him for breakfast, so I downgraded it to porridge and *kande* (a boiled mixture of maize off the cob and pulses),' recalls Mwalimu's former housekeeper, Dorothy Musoga, 74, now living in retirement in Mwanza in a house built for her by Mwalimu....
>
> She was worried...about the future of his family and what she called Mwalimu's 'other children' who loved to share his breakfast. 'With Mwalimu dead, free breakfast for poor villagers will become a thing of the past,' Dorothy reflected.... The poverty of their parents remains, as does the lack of infrastructure at Butiama, which Mwalimu didn't want to transform into an edifice to be envied....
>
> On Saturday, October 23 (1999), when Mwalimu was buried, Butiama may well have started to slip back into oblivion, to become what it once was, an unknown village in the middle of nowhere.... The process may, indeed, have started earlier, with Mwalimu's own house...(which) bears marks of his self-denial. Children fetch water from a public standpipe and their mothers wash clothes in the open. The house itself could do with a fresh coat of paint.... Judging from the relatively wealthier homestead of the chief (nearby), Mwalimu was no more than a peasant....

When I later visited the compound of Mwitongo, where Mwalimu was buried not far from the graves of his parents, only a few insiders and the late Nyerere's close family members had remained, among them his former press secretary Sammy Mdee....

When Chairman Mao was asked what he thought about the French Revolution, a century and a half after it had taken place, he retorted: 'It's too early to say.'

Few in Tanzania can give a better answer about the impact of Nyerere's death. For the poor children of Butiama, however, the days of free breakfast with their beloved grandpa are gone. It is hard to imagine what will follow.[33]

It is indeed hard to imagine what will follow, in a world where there are few such men and women. Nyerere embodied the best that man can achieve in the service of fellow men, but which few are willing to do. He was not a saint, in the religious sense, but may deserve to be called Saint Julius because of his selfless devotion to the poor in the tradition of saints.

He sacrificed so much, yet got so little in return, and did not expect or want anything in return. He just did his job, what he knew had to be done, for his people and others, no matter what the cost. He was the least paid head of state, earning $500 per month, yet one of the most revered; Thomas Sankara of Burkina Faso followed him in his footsteps when he himself became the least paid head of state after Nyerere stepped down. And, instead of living in magnificent splendor, and in the president's official residence, the State House (Ikulu, as we call it), President Nyerere chose to live a humble life in a simple house on the outskirts of the capital in an area called Msasani.

He did not even have a pension to live on when he retired, until parliament hastily voted for one to help sustain him. As *Newsweek* stated soon after he died: "The world has lost a man of principle."[34] Unlike most leaders, including religious leaders, he practiced what he preached. And he admitted his mistakes, a rare quality among leaders, almost all of whom equate such admission with weakness. Yet it's probably the most important quality of leadership on which everything else depends.

Perhaps it is worth remembering that even some of his ardent critics acknowledged his contributions and paid him lasting tribute. Probably no other African scholar kept up a lively debate on the merits of Nyerere's policies as Ali Mazrui did; although he never questioned his commitment and integrity, and powerful intellect, and remained friendly with him until Mwalimu's final days, despite differences between the two. In a tribute to Mwalimu and on the special bonds between the two, Professor Mazrui had a lot to say in his article in *Voices*, Africa Resource Center, entitled, "Nyerere and I":

> In global terms, he was one of the giants of the 20th Century.... While his vision did outpace his victories, and his profundity outweigh his performance, he did bestride this narrow world like an African colossus....
>
> As personalities, what did Julius and I have in common? He was a politician who was sometimes a scholar. I was a scholar who was sometimes a politician.... Nyerere and I were trying to build bridges between Africa and great minds of Western civilisation.... With his concept of Ujamaa, Nyerere also attempted to build bridges between indigenous African thought and modern political ideas....
>
> 'The two top Swahili-speaking intellectuals of the second half of the 20th Century are Julius Nyerere and Ali Mazrui.' That is how I was introduced to an Africanist audience in 1986 when I was on a lecture-tour of the United States to promote my television series: The Africans: A Triple Heritage (BBC-PBS). I regarded the tribute as one of the best compliments I had ever been paid. In reality, Mwalimu Nyerere was much more eloquent as Swahili orator than I although Kiswahili was my mother tongue and not his.
>
> In the month of Nyerere's death (October 1999), the comparison between Mwalimu and I took a sadder form. A number of organisations in South Africa had united to celebrate Africa's Human Rights Day on October 22. Long before he was admitted to hospital, they had invited him to be their high-profile banquet speaker.
>
> When Nyerere was incapacitated with illness, and seemed to be terminally ill, the South Africans turned to Ali Mazrui as his replacement. I was again flattered to have been regarded as Nyerere's replacement. However, the notice was too short, and I was not able to accept the South African invitation.
>
> It is one of the ironies of my life that I have known the early presidents of Uganda and Tanzania far better than I have known the presidents of Kenya (my country). Over the years, Julius Nyerere and I met many times. (Ugandan President) Milton Obote was one of the formative influences of my early life, in spite of our tumultuous relationship....
>
> Let me also refer to Walter Rodney. He was a Guyanese scholar who taught at the University of Dar es Salaam and became one of the most eloquent voices of the left on the campus in Tanzania. When Walter Rodney returned to Guyana, he was assassinated.
>
> Chedi Jagan, on being elected President of Guyana, created a special chair in honour of Walter Rodney. Eventually I was offered the chair and became its first incumbent. My inaugural lecture was on the following topic: 'Comparative Leadership: Walter Rodney, Julius K. Nyerere and Martin Luther King Jr.'
>
> After delivering the lecture, I subsequently met Nyerere one evening in Pennsylvania, USA. I gave him my Walter Rodney lecture. He read it overnight

and commented on it the next morning at breakfast. He promised to send me a proper critique on my Rodney lecture on his return to Dar es Salaam. He never lived long enough to send me the critique.

Nyerere's policies of Ujamaa amounted to a case of Heroic Failure. They were heroic because Tanzania was one of the few African countries, which attempted to find its own route to development instead of borrowing the ideologies of the West. But it was a failure because the economic experiment did not deliver the goods of development.

On the other hand, Nyerere's policies of nation-building amount to a case of Unsung Heroism. With wise and strong leadership, and with brilliant policies of cultural integration, he took one of the poorest countries in the world and made it a proud leader in African affairs and an active member of the global community.

Julius Nyerere was my Mwalimu too. It was a privilege to learn so much from so great a man.[35]

A man of high integrity and an enormous and astonishing intellect, he was one of the most exalted among men. But he was also one of the most humble. He was, indeed, a man of the people. Such is the mark of true genius, a rare breed among men. As former American President Jimmy Carter said: "Julius Nyerere should be remembered as one of the greatest leaders of this century."[36] It is a fitting tribute, although somewhat of an understatement. The world has, in fact, produced only a few such men and women in a span of centuries.

And he had few peers on the African continent who could equal his stature; a point underscored by Ali Mazrui in another tribute to Nyerere at Cornell University, although he disagreed with him on a number of fundamental issues. He last saw Nyerere when both were among the main speakers in different forums during the inauguration of Nigerian President Olusegun Obasanjo in May 1999. As he stated in his lecture at Cornell, also published in Kenya's *Daily Nation*:

> Most Western judges of Julius Nyerere have concentrated on his economic policies and their failures. Ujamaa and villagisation have been seen as forces of economic retardation, which kept Tanzania backward for at least another decade.
>
> Not enough commentators have paid attention to Nyerere's achievements in nation-building. He gave Tanzania a sense of national consciousness and a spirit of national purpose. One of the poorest countries in the world found itself one of the major actors on the world scene. Nyerere's policies of making Kiswahili the national language of Tanzania deepened this sense of Tanzania's

national consciousness and cultural pride....

Above all, Nyerere as president was a combination of deep intellect and high integrity. Leopold Senghor's intellect was as deep as Nyerere's, but was Senghor's integrity as high as Nyerere's? Nelson Mandela's integrity was probably higher than Nyerere's, but was Mandela's intellect as deep as Nyerere's?

Some East African politicians might have been more intelligent than Nyerere. Others might have been more ethical than Nyerere. But Julius K. Nyerere was in a class by himself in the combination of ethical standards and intellectual power. In the combination of high thinking and high ethics, no other East African politician was in the same league.

He and I deeply disagreed on the merits of Ujamaa. He and I once disagreed on East African federation. I thought his socialist policies harmed East African integration. He and I disagreed on the Nigerian civil war. He and I disagreed on the issue of Zanzibar. I thought Zanzibar was forced into a marriage, which was not of its own choosing.

And yet Nyerere and I were committed to the proposition that patriotic Africans could disagree and still be equally patriotic. I saw him in Abuja in Nigeria, just before the inauguration of President Olusegun Obasanjo late in May 1999. Julius Nyerere and I gossiped in Kiswahili. He looked well - deceptively well, considering his illness.

He and I were keynote speakers at a workshop to inaugurate Nigeria to a new era of democracy in 1999. We were voices from East Africa at a major West African event. We were voices of Pan-Africanism on the eve of the new millennium. Nyerere's voice was one of the most eloquent voices of the 20th Century. It was a privilege for me to stand side-by-side with such a person to mark a momentous event in no less a country than our beloved Nigeria.[37]

A man whom Mazrui also once hailed as "the most original thinker in English-speaking Africa," a tribute he also paid to Senghor with regard to Francophone Africa,[38] Nyerere will always remain an inspiration to millions, including some of his critics.

Mazrui, himself a leading critic of Nyerere's policies yet an admirer of Nyerere's intellect and integrity, drew fire through the years from some of the most vociferous defenders of Nyerere and his policies.

They included the late Dr. Walter Rodney from Guyana who taught at the University of Dar es Salaam when I was a reporter at the *Daily News*; other professors and students at the university as well as a number of Tanzanians including some reporters at the *Daily News* and *The Nationalist* in Dar es Salaam.

To many of them, his criticism of Tanzania's egalitarian policies in a nation of poor peasants and workers amounted to a case of Tanzaphobia by one of Africa's leading academics, and probably the most well-known in international circles besides his nemesis Wole Soyinka.

I also disagreed with Mazrui on a number of issues, although I did not have the visceral hatred for him that was obvious among some of his leftist critics, of which I wasn't one. I was simply a nationalist and Pan-Africanist, neither to the right nor to the left, as I still am today, although I have sympathized with leftist causes more than I have with those on the right, if at all.

When I was a student at Tambaza High School in standard 14 (Form VI) in 1970, I remember reading in one of Tanzania's two major daily newspapers, *The Nationalist*, a letter to the editor - Ben Mkapa, later my editor at the *Daily News*, and president of Tanzania (1995 - 2005) - from Professor Ali Mazrui. It was a passionate defence of his patriotism in response to his critics who felt that he was highly critical of Tanzania's policies out of sheer spite and hatred, and not out of genuine commitment to the well-being of the country.

He responded by saying that he loved Tanzania, and that Tanzania meant a lot to him. He went on say that he spent part of his childhood in Tanzania, in what was then Zanzibar, and partly attended school in Tanzania (then Tanganyika) when he was growing up. He said he went to school in Moshi, in Kilimanjaro Region in northeastern Tanzania, and that Tanzania will always be important to him.

The letter may have elicited some sympathy for him from some of the readers, but many of his critics were probably impressed by none of this.

Some of them were brutally frank in their assessment of the renowned Kenyan professor; for example, Kusai Khamisa, a senior reporter at our newspaper, now deceased, said "Mazrui has a pathological hatred of Tanzania." And one senior Tanzanian diplomat whom I knew said "Ali Mazrui has done everything possible to destroy Tanzania. I have been tempted several times to write a crtique of his writings."

I remember talking to Philip Ochieng' - a Kenyan himself - one day in 1972 when we worked together at the *Daily News*, and asking him what he thought about Ali Mazrui. I brought up the subject, and knowing Philip's strong political views, I wanted to hear what he had to say about it.

A fiery Marxist, yet who years later was appointed editor of the capitalist government-owned *Kenya Times* under President Daniel arap Moi after he returned to Kenya, he dismissed Mazrui as a very dangerous academic. No capital offense, but criticism of government, the kind Mazrui was known for even if just as a scholar engaged in objective evaluation and analaysis of ideas, has sent people to the gallows in many African countries.

Others have been summarily executed, shot on the spot, or simply "disappeared." As Mazrui himself says, he almost got killed by Idi Amin in Uganda for criticizing him. I remember reading an article Mazrui wrote after he fled Uganda and when Amin was busy expelling Asians, including Ugandan citizens who just happened to be of Asian origin. It was entitled, "When Spain Expelled the Moors," and incurred the wrath of the dictator, obviously after someone read it to him and told him what Mazrui meant by that. Amin had only a standard two - second grade - education and could hardly read or write. Mazrui taught at Makerere University in Kampala, Uganda.

But such blunt assessment of pro-capitalist academics like Mazrui and others was not unusual in socialist-oriented Tanzania among leftists like Philip Ochieng'. Nor was criticism of the West.

Although I myself was a strong admirer of Nyerere and other African leaders such as Nkrumah because of their egalitarian policies and Pan-African commitment, and was not enamored of the West, I was sometimes criticized by some of my colleagues on the editorial staff at the *Daily News* for wearing a necktie almost everyday; as did two other reporters, Judicate Shoo and Emmanuel Lenga. One day, Philip, who always wore a short-sleeved shirt or a dashiki, lifted my tie and said, half-jokingly, "Godfrey, you're tied to the West," as he shook it.

That was ridiculous. I was tied to the West as much as he was when he enjoyed drinks imported from the West, which he did, and wore Western clothes, minus a tie; and as much as he enjoyed Western music. Philip loved humming Western tunes including "Guantanamera," his favourite, which he often whistled in our editorial office, punctuating the tune with the song's name. The name Philip itself tied him to the West - not just to the Biblical homeland - just as much, and like mine, of course. So did President Nyerere's first name, Julius!

Just remember Mobutu, with his full African name and indigenization policy of "Authenticity," complete with a leopard-skin hat, and a traditional cane he carried and which is so common among African chiefs and other traditional rulers as a symbol of authority. In 1971, he ordered all names in the country changed to African names. He also "indigenized" the economy by raiding national coffers for himself and giving property - seized from foreigners - to his cronies and family members who had also amassed wealth by stealing from the masses.

Now, contrast that with Patrice Lumumba who wore Western suits and a necktie. Who was more tied to the West?

Leopold Senghor espoused Negritude - about which Wole Soyinka said "a tiger does not have to proclaim its tigritude" - yet he was unabashedly Francophile and proud to be a "black Frenchman."

Dr. Milton Obote wore Western suits and a necktie, besides African safari suits also worn by Dr. Kenneth Kaunda who stopped wearing Western suits and replaced them with what came to be popularly known as Kaunda style. Was Obote tied to the West? In fact Philip Ochieng' admitted, even in some of his writings, that Obote was his hero second only to Nyerere.

And what about Robert Mugabe, and Samora Machel, admirers of Chairman Mao, and Marxist firebrands until they were tempered by harsh economic realities, who also wore Western suits and neckties? Were they tied to the West? During the land crisis in Zimbabwe in the late 1990s and beyond, Mugabe showed the whole world how much he was tied to the West!

But that is the twisted logic of some leftists, although many of their counterparts are Westerners and wear Western suits and neckties, just like the politburo members in the former Soviet Union and her satellites, as well as ordinary citizens in those countries, did.

It is ironic that many people in Third World countries are highly critical of the industrialized West - and for good reasons in many cases, although sometimes out of sheer spite - yet they want to live like Westerners, admire the Western life style, and ape the consumption proclivities of the West.

Critical of the West as Philip was, I still remember that some reporters on our editorial staff did not see much virtue, if any, in such criticism by him because of his Western tastes, including his social life however personal that was; as it indeed was. As senior reporter Reginald Mhango - later managing editor of *The Guardian* - once asked, loudly, in our editorial office about Philip's dating preferences: "Why just white women?"

Mhango may have had a valid point. So did Philip, of course, who could have retorted had he been within earshot: "So what? That's none of your business"; just as it was none of his that I wore a necktie, which "tied me to the West," as he saw it.

Whaever the case, Philip Ochieng', one of Africa's most prominent journalists and Kenya's best known, remained an unrepentant Marxist despite the collapse of communism and renunciation of Marxism-Leninism as a state ideology by almost all the countries which had adopted it, except North Korea, ruled by Stalinist hardliners, and Cuba under the internationalist Castro.

But we agreed on one thing: Nyerere was a great leader. And he was not just Tanzania's, but Africa's leader.

He first wanted to unite East African countries, but failed to do so. Yet that was not his fault. Some of his critics blamed him for that. They include Ali Mazrui who blamed Nyerere's - hence Tanzania's - policies for the failure of the proposed federation.

But that is not why the three East African countries of Kenya, Uganda, and Tanganyika failed to unite. They did not unite because of nationalism; which is also the main reason why regional integration in Africa has failed, to answer one of the questions Mazrui raised in his memorial lecture at Cornell University in October 1999, in which he paid tribute to President Julius Nyerere.

Nationalism triumphed over Pan-Africanism in the East African context because Kenya and Uganda did not want to surrender their sovereignties to a macro-national state in which they would be submerged. Only Nyerere, among the three East African leaders, was ready to do so. Nyerere even offered to delay Tanganyika's independence so that the three East African countries could attain sovereign status on the same day and unite under one government. And among the three, Kenya was the least enthusiastic.

At a meeting in Nairobi, Kenya, in June 1963, the three East African leaders - Kenyatta, Nyerere, and Obote - signed a declaration of intent to form a federation before the end of the year. Many people were excited about this, and even songs were composed heralding the dawn of a new era. I remember a song in Kiswahili which was often played in the early and mid-1960s on the radio in Tanganyika and Kenya, called "Shirikisho la Afrika ya Mashariki,"which means the Federation of East Africa.

It was sung by one of Kenya's and East Africa's most popular musicians and guitarists, Peter Tsotsi, originally from Northern Rhodesia, which is Zambia today. Others sang the same song.

Other famous musicians and guitar players in Kenya during those days and in the following years included Daudi Kabaka, originally from Uganda, and Fadhili Williams.

But the federation was never consummated, in spite of all the optimism we had.

It was expected that the president of the East African Federation - Federal Republic of East Africa or whatever - would be Jomo Kenyatta, in deference to Mzee, the Grand Old Man; and Julius Nyerere would be vice president. But Kenya also wanted the foreign minister of the East African federation to be a Kenyan, probably Tom Mboya. Uganda would therefore have been frozen out of all the three top positions; hardly a basis for unity.

And, obviously, the extortionate demands by Kenya were deliberately intended to frustrate Nyerere's - and to a smaller degree, Obote's - efforts to unite the three East African countries. Therefore Kenyan leaders would, perhaps, have agreed to unite with Uganda and Tanganyika only if they were going to dominate the federation.

Kenya also did not want to lose its dominant position as the most developed and industrialized country in East Africa. During British colonial rule, Nairobi was virtually the capital of East Africa. It was the headquarters of the East African Common Services Organisation (EACSO) - railways and harbors, posts and telecommunications, airways, currency board, research facilities and much more. It was also the largest and most developed city in East Africa.

And of all the East African countries, Kenya had the largest number of European settlers, about 66,000 and mostly British including members of the British aristocracy. They invested heavily in Kenya and tried to develop its economy because they saw it as an outpost of Britain which one day would become an independent state under white rule like South Africa, Australia and New Zealand; a dream white settlers in Rhodesia, now Zimbabwe, also tried to pursue. That is why Lord Delamere, Kenya's first governor, called it "White Man's Country."

Had Kenya agreed to unite with Uganda and Tanganyika to form a federation, it would have to be an equal among equals; would have been required to contribute a bigger share to the federal budget because of its relatively strong economy; and would have to make other sacrifices - in terms of revenue sharing and removing tariffs to import more goods from Uganda and Tanganyika - in order to help the two weaker economies catch up. And this was just too much for the Kenyan leadership. Kenya, not East Africa, came first, because of nationalism.

Uganda was also a major problem. Dr. Milton Obote wanted to form the federation probably as much as Nyerere did, and even spoke out against the dissolution of the Central African Federation of Rhodesia (Northern Rhodesia and Southern Rhodesia) and Nyasaland. He was the only African leader to do so. He believed that had the Central African Federation (which was formed in 1953 and dissolved in 1963) emerged from colonial rule as a single entity, it would have been a powerful African supra-nation and a major step towards continental unity.

But Uganda had serious internal problems because of strong opposition to the national government led by Obote. The strongest opposition came from the Buganda kingdom, virtually a state within a state, whose leaders were determined to reclaim its lost glory as an independent nation as it was before the advent of colonial rule like the Ashanti in Ghana. Other traditional strongholds in Uganda were also opposed to central authority.

If all these kingdoms - Buganda, Ankole, Bunyoro, and the princedom of Busoga as well as other traditional centers of authority such as the Teso and the Acholi - were not ready to surrender power to the national government in Kampala; then one would certainly not have expected them to do so to an even more distant authority at the federal level of the three East African countries.

In terms of national integration, Uganda faced the toughest problem among all the three countries. Nyerere himself conceded that much, despite his unflinching determination to unite all the countries in the region, a goal he pursued until his death.

Many Ugandan leaders also invoked the constitution saying it did not allow them to surrender their country's sovereignty to any other authority; a provision that was included to appease the Buganda kingdom and others opposed to any further diminution of their authority. The national government itself was more than enough for them.

Yet, if the Ugandan leaders were serious about forming an East African federation, they could have changed their constitution and included a provision requiring Uganda to renounce her sovereign status in favor of union as the Ghananian constitution of March 1960 did, committing Ghana to full or partial renunciation of her sovereignty to achieve African unity.

Regarding Tanzania's socialist policies as an obstacle to federation, we need not look further to see that it was in fact Kenya, not Tanzania, which was an anomaly among the three countries and therefore the main obstacle to federation.

Both Nyerere and Obote were socialist-oriented even far back then, in 1963, before they proclaimed their socialist policies, while Kenyatta was not. Therefore it was Kenya's capitalist policies, which wrecked the proposed federation, as Nyerere and Obote moved closer ideologically and in terms of policy formulation, eventually promulgating socialist policies.

Tanzania issued the Arusha Declaration in February 1967, and Uganda the Common Man's Charter in October 1969. But even they failed to unite, without Kenya, in spite of their common socialist policies and one-party states. Kenya also became a one-party state in 1969 following the banning of the opposition Kenya People's Union (KPU) led by former vice president Oginga Odinga.

The three countries even had a common market, a common currency, and common services - including posts and telecommunications, railways and harbors, the East African Airways (EAA), and research institutes - inherited from the British and which would have formed a solid foundation for a federal state. Still, they failed to unite, because of nationalism.

There was also the Nyerere factor, a potent factor, especially among Kenyans who wanted to dominate the federation but who also feared that the charismatic and highly influential Tanganyikan leader would emerge as the dominant political figure on the scene and become president of the East African Federation; a dreadful prospect for nationalist-minded Kenyans.

There was also, among the national leaders of Kenya and Uganda, fear of losing power and status to a higher authority at the federal level. For example, not all the cabinet members in the three national governments would have become cabinet members in the federal government, or even ambassadors. This was one of the strongest disincentives to consummation of the union, and all professions by them in different forums - including diplomatic conclaves - in support of East African unity was no more than empty rhetoric.

But in fairness, we must also admit that there were some people in the government of Tanganyika who felt the same way as their counterparts did in Kenya and Uganda. There was, however, one fundamental difference. Tanganyika under Nyerere was committed to federation. Kenya and Uganda were not.

Another reason why the three East African countries did not form a federation was the unwillingness among Kenyan and Ugandan leaders to lose platforms in international forums where their countries would no longer be sovereign entities. They would cease to exist. Thus, instead of having three East African governments, each speaking for its own country at the United Nations, the World Bank and other international organizations and institutions, there would - under federation - be only one government; which was unthinkable.

That is why the federation was never formed. And none of those factors had anything to do with Tanganyika, the strongest proponent of East African integration for which Nyerere was prepared to sacrifice so much, including giving up Tanganyika's status as a separate entity.

Even if Tanganyika and Uganda had chosen the capitalist path, capitalist Kenya would still not have united with them. And Uganda would have continued to rationalize her opposition to such a union on constitutional grounds.

Obote supported the unification of the three East African

countries, unlike most of his colleagues in Uganda. But when in 1964 the Ugandan government and parliament invoked the constitution to justify their opposition to federation, with Kenya already opposed to such a merger, it became obvious that the union could not be formed even under the best of circumstances: similar political and economic systems - neither Tanzania nor Uganda had gone socialist then, and Tanzania did not become a *de jure* one-party state until 1965.

And the constitutional argument advanced by Uganda was not a very clever one, as we showed earlier. Constitutions can be amended and even abrogated.

The failure of the three East African countries to unite was one of the Nyerere's biggest disappointments; a point he underscored in an interview with James McKinley of *The New York Times* in his home village of Butiama in August 1996, more than 30 years after that abortive attempt, and 11 years after he voluntarily stepped down from the presidency.

Looking back on his political career, he said his greatest failure was that although he managed to form a union with Zanzibar in 1964 to create Tanzania, he never succeeded in persuading neighboring countries to form a larger entity, a move, he said, that would have made the region a powerhouse.[39] Yet, he succeeded in uniting a country of almost 130 different tribes into a cohesive and stable nation unparalleled on the African continent. And in another unprecedented move, he not only succeeded in uniting two independent countries, but in forming the only union in the history of post-colonial Africa, and which has survived for more than 40 years.

His unsurpassed skills in nation-building were clearly evident, not only across tribal but also racial lines, creating a political entity that is virtually indistinguishable from an organic whole. In terms of racial harmony, Tanzania is one of the very few countries in Africa to have achieved that. And it is probably the only one where non-black candidates - of European, Asian, and Arab descent - never lost elections to black candidates in predominantly black constituencies.

There was, for example, Derek Bryceson, a Tanzanian of British descent who always won elections against black candidates to represent Kilosa District in parliament. He was also the only white elected official on the entire continent representing an overwhelmingly black district in parliament, and held a number of cabinet posts under President Nyerere for many years, mostly as minister of agriculture. When he died in a British hospital in 1980, his body was flown back to Tanzania for burial after a state funeral. Thousands of people went to the airport to receive the body, and thousands more lined the streets of Dar es Salaam to pay their last respects as the vehicle carrying his body in a convoy of cars passed by. He was one of the most popular and respected leaders of Tanzania.

Amir H. Jamal, of Indian descent, was another very popular and highly respected leader and technocrat who represented Morogoro District in parliament and, like Bryceson, never lost an election against black candidates in a predominantly black constituency. He also held several senior cabinet posts - finance; commerce and industries; development and economic planning, and others including ambassadorial - for many years since independence.

He also served as chairman of the Board of Governors of the International Monetary Fund (IMF) when he was Tanzania's minister of economic planning. He died in 1995 in Vancouver, Canada. Speaking at his funeral in Dar es Salaam, Nyerere remembered him as a colleague and compatriot, in a moving speech, and on one of the saddest occasions in the country's history.

Both Bryceson and Jamal were also veterans of the independence struggle. And there were many others - white, Asian, Arab - in different leadership positions and other posts working together with indigenous Africans, as they still do today including some cabinet members.

None of this would have been possible had it not been for President Julius Nyerere or another leader of such high caliber capable of uniting members of different tribes and races into a cohesive entity. And he inspired those who followed in his footsteps, President Ali Hassan Mwinyi and President Benjamin Mkapa, to pursue the same policies of tolerance, harmony, and peaceful co-existence; although after his death, agitation for greater autonomy - euphemism for independence in this context - in Zanzibar gained momentum, and ethnoregional rivalries and racial hostilities began to surface on an unprecedented scale.

But he still left behind a stable nation, relatively speaking, and continues to inspire millions of Tanzanians to close ranks and maintain national unity.

In the pantheon of African leaders, he is one of those who continue to inspire millions across the continent. And his Pan-African commitment was no mere rhetoric, unlike that of most of his colleagues. He meant what he said, and did it. For example, the liberation struggle in southern Africa would probably have taken a different turn had it not been for his commitment and sacrifice. And tens of thousands of refugees from other African countries were given citizenship through the decades when he was president.

In the early eighties alone, almost 100,000 people, mostly from Rwanda and Burundi, became Tanzanian citizens. And he extended his hospitality to others who were equally embraced with open arms. Thousands of refugees from Mozambique during the liberation war in the Portuguese colony also became citizens of Tanzania because of Nyerere's magnanimous policies.

And he continued to make sacrifices for fellow Africans across the continent until his last days; his relentless effort to help resolve the conflict in Burundi being only one example. When Dr. Kenneth Kaunda was jailed by President Frederick Chiluba for allegedly plotting to overthrow him, Nyerere intervened and helped get him out of jail.

When Olusegun Obasanjo was imprisoned by Nigerian military dictator Sani Abacha, Nyerere worked relentlessly to help free him. After he was freed, Obasanjo said Nyerere was the first person outside Nigeria to call him, and told him he was sorry he did not work hard enough to help get him out of prison; testament to his humility.

At Nyerere's funeral in Dar es Salaam, President Obasanjo nearly whispered as he recalled how Nyerere worked hard to free him from prison where he was serving a life sentence - reduced to 15 years - for allegedly trying to overthrow the government of military dictator Sani Abacha: "He was the first non-Nigerian who called me when I was freed, and he told me he was afraid he hadn't done enough."[40]

His death will never be forgotten by many people, including

me. Nyerere's death will remain memorable to me in another respect, although this is only coincidental. He entered Edinburgh University in Scotland in October 1949 where he earned a master's degree in economics and history, and returned to Tanganyika in October 1952. That was the same year, 1949, and the same month of October, in which I was born in Kigoma in western Tanganyika under British colonial rule.

And he died almost exactly 50 years later, on October 14, 1999, 10 days after my 50th birthday on October 4th. That is not the best way to remember one's birthday, yet, because of this, I will never forget when he died.

He was mourned around the world, by the most humble and the most exalted; true testament to his greatness as a selfless leader who put the people first, including those groaning under apartheid and other oppressive regimes, black and white. Without his commitment and sacrifice, Tanzania would probably not have survived as a stable and united country.

And that pretty much sums up what ails Africa today: lack of good leadership more than anything else. It is lack of effective, dedicated leadership, which led to the destruction of Somalia as a nation, the first African country to "disappear" from the map. It is also lack of good leadership, which explains why other African countries dissolved in anarchy, torn by civil wars: Rwanda, Burundi, Congo-Kinshasa, Congo-Brazzaville, Liberia, and Sierra Leone.

That is also why other forms of civil strife in different parts of the continent have become a prominent feature of the political landscape and national life.

One can't help but wonder what would have happened in all these countries if they had leaders of Nyerere's and Mandela's caliber, genuinely committed to the well-being of their people, instead of being only interested in how much they are going to steal from them, and how they are going to oppress them and favor members of their tribes and sell their countries to outsiders. As Nyerere said in Accra, Ghana, where he was invited to participate in celebrations marking the 40th anniversary of Ghana's independence in March 1997:

> We must not allow the future of Africa to be determined by those outside Africa. This is 1997 not 1887 - three years away from the 21st century. We

must determine our own destiny. We've got to empower ourselves through unity to determine the fate of our continent...

Today we have African leaders who have simply looted their countries and their countries have gone to the dogs. We don't need those men...but we do need leadership. We need government that works and we need a hard-core of people who are willing to work hard and contribute to their country's welfare.[41]

It is a fitting tribute that Africans from different countries across the continent and other people elsewhere decided to institute a continental award known as the Nyerere Prize for Ethics, proposed by the Independent Commission on the Third Millennium for Africa based in Cotonou, Benin.

The award will go to leaders who have demonstrated outstanding ethical conduct, in honor of the late Mwalimu Julius Nyerere because of his exemplary leadership, which earned him the title, "The Conscience of Africa." Supporters of the project include African governments, the United Nations, and other different organizations and institutions.

But, commendable as the project is, who is really going to get this award? Who deserves it on this beleaguered continent of brutal autocrats and kleptocrats who don't mind bleeding their people to death in more than one way? It is a continent mangled, crippled, and bled by the very same leaders who are going to claim the award "in the name of the people." As Nyerere himself said not long before he died: "Africa is in a mess."

The award may, indeed, have been established in vain; hardly a fitting tribute to a man who died trying to bring peace to one of the most embattled parts of our continent, the Great Lakes region of East-central Africa, and elsewhere.

Although he is gone, his ideals will always be with us. And they will continue to inspire us in our quest for peace and stability, justice and equality, for which he lived and died. It is ideals which can be achieved through unity, without which no country can survive, let alone thrive. But they will remain unattainable ideals if the building blocks for African unity are fragmented by ethnic conflicts and other forms of civil strife.

Many countries have been pulverized from within, and several others continue to sustain crippling blows because of their inability or unwillingness to address one vital issue: There can be no peace without stability, and no stability without justice and equality for all. And that entails, not only guaranteeing freedom of expression as a fundamental democratic right, but equal participation in the political process and in policy formulation and implementation on consensus basis at all levels of government. It also requires equitable redistribution of wealth to all regions and groups in order to contain and defuse ethnic and regional tensions and rivalries. Most of these are caused by discrimination; hardly a basis for unity. Fortunately, we were able to avoid these problems in Tanzania because of Nyerere's leadership.

Growing up in Tanganyika in the fifties and sixties was a memorable experience for me. I was born under colonial rule 12 years before independence. I grew up not only in an independent but a united republic. When Tanganyika won independence from Britain on December 9, 1961, I was 12 years old and did not have the slightest idea of what was going to happen in only two years. Even grown-ups involved or interested in politics did not have any idea that we would be living in a new country within so short a time.

On April 26, 1964, Tanganyika united with Zanzibar. The new country was called the Union of Tanganyika and Zanzibar until October 29 the same year when it was renamed the United Republic of Tanzania.

It has been one long journey since then, and we still have a long way to go towards unity across the continent. But achieving this noble objective entails, first and foremost, conflict resolution in Africa. It is a goal Nyerere was trying to achieve when his life came to an end, an end which also marked the beginning of a new era towards the end of the twentieth century. As he said in Accra, Ghana, on March 6, 1997, in a speech celebrating Ghana's 40th independence anniversary, his generation fought for independence. It is now for this generation to unite Africa. His speech was entitled, "Africa Must Unite":

> Forty years ago the people of Ghana celebrated the raising of the flag of their independence for the first time. Throughout Africa people celebrated - in solidarity with Ghana but also for themselves. For the liberation of Africa was a single struggle with many fronts. Ghana's independence from colonial rule in 1957 was recognised for what it was: the beginning of the end of colonialism for the whole of Africa. For centuries we had been oppressed and humiliated as

Africans. We were hunted and enslaved as Africans, as we were colonized as Africans.

The humiliation of Africans became the glorification of others. So we felt our African-ness. We knew that we were one people, and that we had one destiny regardless of the artificial boundaries, which the colonialists had invented. Since we were humiliated as Africans we had to be liberated as Africans.

So forty years ago we recognised your independence as the first triumph in Africa's struggle for freedom and dignity. It was the first success of our demand to be accorded the international respect, which is accorded free peoples. Ghana was the beginning, our first liberated zone. Thirty-seven years later in 1994 - we celebrated our final triumph when apartheid was crushed and Nelson Mandela was installed as the president of South Africa. Africa's long struggle for freedom was over.

But Ghana was more than just the beginning. Ghana inspired and deliberately spearheaded the independence struggle for the rest of Africa.

I was a student at Edinburgh University when Kwame Nkrumah was released from prison to be Leader of Government Business in his first elected government. The deportment of the Gold Coast students changed. The way they carried themselves up - they way they talked to us and others, the way they looked at the world at large, changed overnight. They even looked different.

They were not arrogant, they were not overbearing, they were not aloof, but they were proud. Already they felt free and they exuded that quiet pride of self-confidence of freedom without which humanity is incomplete.

And so eight years later when the Gold Coast became independent, Kwame Nkrumah invited us, the leaders of the various liberation movements in Africa, to come and celebrate with you. I was among the many invited. Then Nkrumah made a famous declaration, that Ghana's independence was meangingless unless the whole of Africa was liberated from colonial rule. Kwame Nkrumah went into action almost immediately.

In the following year he called the liberation movements to Ghana to discuss a common strategy for the liberation of the continent from colonialism. In preparation for the African Peoples' Conference, those of us in East and Central Africa met in Mwanza, Tanganyika, to discuss our possible contribution to the forthcoming conference. That conference lit the liberation torch throughout colonial Africa.

Kwame Nkrumah was your leader, but he was our leader too: For he was an African leader. People are not gods. Even the best have their faults, and the faults of the great can be very big. So Kwame Nkrumah had his faults. But he was great in a purely positive sense. He was a visionary. He thought big, but he thought big for Ghana and its people and for Africa and its people. He had a great dream for Africa and its people. He had the well-being of our people at heart. He was no looter. He did not have a Swiss bank account. He died poor. Shakespeare wrote that the evil that men do lives after them, but the good is often interred with their bones.

Five years later, in May 1963, thirty-two independent African states met in

Addis Ababa, founded the Organisation of African Unity (OAU), and established the liberation committee of the new organisation, charging it with the duty of coordinating the liberation struggle in those parts of Africa still under colonial rule.

The following year, 1964, the OAU met in Cairo. That Cairo summit is remembered mainly for the declaration of the heads of state of independent Africa to respect the borders inherited from colonialism. The principle of non-interference in the internal affairs of member states of the OAU had been enshrined in the charter itself; respect for the borders inherited from colonialism comes from the Cairo Declaration of 1964 (the resolution was Nyerere's idea and he introduced it at the Cairo summit). In 1965, the OAU met in Accra. That summit is not well remembered as the founding summit in 1963, or the Cairo summit of 1964.

The fact that Kwame Nkrumah did not last long as head of state of Ghana after that summit may have contributed to the comparative obscurity of that important summit. But I want to suggest that the reason why we do not talk much about that summit is probably psychological: it was a failure. That failure still haunts us today.

The founding fathers of the OAU had set themselves two major objectives: the total liberation of our continent from colonialism and settler minorities, and the unity of Africa. The first objective was expressed through the immediate establishment of the Liberation Committee by the founding summit. The second objective was expressed in the name of the organisation - it is the Organisation of African Unity.

Critics could say that the charter itself, with its great emphasis on the sovereign independence of each member state, combined with the Cairo Declaration on the sanctity of the inherited borders, makes it look like the 'Organisation of African Disunity.' But that would be carrying criticism too far and ignoring the objective reasons which led to the principles of non-interference in the Cairo Declaration.

What the founding fathers - certainly a hard-core of them - had in mind was genuine desire to move Africa towards greater unity. We loathed the balkanization of the continent into small non-viable states, most of which had borders, which did not make ethnic or geographical sense. The Cairo Declaration was prompted by a profound realisation of the absurdity of those borders.

It was quite clear that some adventurers would try to change those borders by force of arms. Indeed, it was already happening. Ethiopia and Somalia were at war over inherited borders. Kwame Nkrumah was opposed to balkanization as much as he was opposed to colonialism in Africa. To him and to a number of us, the two - balkanization and colonization - were twins. Genuine liberation of Africa had to attack both twins. A struggle against colonialism must go hand in hand with a struggle against the balkanization of Africa.

Kwame Nkrumah was the great crusader for African unity. He wanted the Accra summit of 1965 to establish a union government for the whole of independent Africa. But we failed. The one minor reason is that Kwame, like all great believers, underestimated the degree of suspicion and animosity, which his crusading passion had created among a substantial number of his fellow heads of state. The major reason was linked to the first: already too many of us had a vested interest in keeping Africa divided.

Prior to independence of Tanganyika, I had been advocating that East African countries should federate and then achieve independence as a single political unit. I had said publicly that I was willing to delay Tanganyika's independence in order to enable all three-mainland countries to achieve their independence together as a single federated state.

I made the suggestion because of my fear, proved correct by later events, that it would be very difficult to unite our countries if we let them achieve independence separately.

Once you multiply national anthems, national flags and national passports, seats at the United Nations, and individuals entitled to 21-gun salute, not to speak of a host of ministers, prime ministers, and envoys, you will have a whole army of powerful people with vested interests in keeping Africa balkanized. That was what Nkrumah encountered in 1965.

After the failure to establish the union government at the Accra summit of 1965, I heard one head of state express with relief that he was happy to be returning home to his country still head of state. To this day I cannot tell whether he was serious or joking. But he may well have been serious, because Kwame Nkrumah was very serious and the fear of a number of us to lose our precious status was quite palpable.

But I never believed that the 1965 Accra summit would have established a union government for Africa. When I say that we failed, that is not what I mean, for that clearly was an unrealistic objective for a single summit. What I mean is that we did not even discuss a mechanism for pursuing the objective of a politically united Africa. We had a Liberation Committee already. We should have at least had a Unity Committee or undertaken to establish one. We did not. And after Kwame Nkrumah was removed from the African political scene nobody took up the challenge again.

So my remaining remarks have a confession and a plea. The confession is that we of the first generation leaders of independent Africa have not pursued the objective of African unity with the vigour, commitment and sincerity that it deserves. Yet that does not mean that unity is now irrelevant.

Does the experience of the last three or four decades of Africa's independence dispel the need for African unity? With our success in the liberation struggle, Africa today has 53 independent states, 21 more than those, which met in Addis Ababa in May 1963. If numbers were horses, Africa would be riding high! Africa would be the strongest continent in the world, for it occupies more seats in the UN General Assembly than any other continent. Yet the reality is that ours is the poorest and weakest continent in the world. And our weakness is pathetic. Unity will not end our weakness, but until we unite, we cannot even begin to end that weakness.

So this is my plea to the new generation of African leaders and African people: Work for unity with firm conviction that without unity there is no future for Africa. That is, of course, assuming that we still want to have a place under the sun.

I reject the glorification of the nation-state, which we have inherited from colonialism, and the artificial nations we are trying to forge from that inheritance. We are all Africans trying very hard to be Ghanaians or Tanzanians. Fortunately for Africa we have not been completely successful. The outside world hardly recognises our Ghanaian-ness or Tanzanian-ness. What the outside world recognises about us is our African-ness.

Hitler was a German, Mussolini was an Italian, Franco was a Spaniard, Salazaar was a Portuguese, Stalin was a Russian or a Georgian. Nobody expected Churchill to be ashamed of Hitler. He was probably ashamed of Chamberlain. Nobody expected Charles de Gaulle to be ashamed of Hitler. He was probably ashamed of the complicity of Vichy. It is Germans, and Italians and Spaniards and Portuguese who feel uneasy about those dictators in their respective countries.

Not so in Africa. Idi Amin was in Uganda, but of Africa, Jean Bokassa was in Central Africa, but of Africa. Some of the dictators are still active in their respective countries, but they are all of Africa. They are all Africans, and all are perceived by the outside world as Africans. When I travel outside Africa the description of me as former president of Tanzania is a fleeting affair. It does not stick. Apart from the ignorant who sometimes asked me whether Tanzania was Johannesburg, even to those who knew better, what stuck in the minds of my hosts was the fact of my African-ness. So I had to answer questions about the atrocities of the Amins and the Bokassas of Africa.

Mrs. Gandhi did not have to answer questions about the atrocities of Asia. Nor does Fidel Castro have to answer about the atrocities of the Somozas of Latin America. But when I travel or meet foreigners, I have to answer questions about Somalia, Liberia, Rwanda, Burundi and Zaire, as in the past I used to answer questions about Mozambique, Angola, Zimbabwe, Namibia or South Africa.

And the way I was perceived is the way most of my fellow heads of state were perceived. And that is the way you are all being perceived. So accepting the fact that we are Africans gives you a much more worthwhile challenge than the current desperate attempts to fossilize Africa into the wounds inflicted upon it by the vultures of imperialism....

Reject the return to the tribe. There is richness of culture out there, which we must do everything we can to preserve and share. But it is utter madness to think that if these artificial, non-viable states, which we are trying to create, are broken up into tribal components and we turn those into nation-states, we might save ourselves.

That kind of political and social atavism spells catastrophe for Africa. It would be the end of any kind of genuine development for Africa. It would fossilize Africa into a worse state than the one in which we are. The future of Africa, the modernization of Africa that has a place in the 21st century is linked up with its decolonization and detribalization. Tribal atavism would be giving up any hope for Africa. And of all the sins that Africa can commit, the sin of despair would be the most unforgivable.

Reject the nonsense of dividing African people into Anglophones, Francophones and Lusophones. This attempt to divide our people according to the language of their former colonial masters must be rejected with the firmness and utter contempt that it richly deserves. The natural owners of those wonderful languages are busy building a united Europe. But Europe is strong, even without unity. It has less need for unity and strength that comes from unity than Africa....

The second phase of the liberation of Africa is going to be much harder than the first. But it can be done. It must done. Empower Africa through unity, and Africa shall be free, strong and prosperous....

A new generation of self-respecting Africans should spit in the face of anybody who suggests that our continent should remain divided and fossilized....in order to satisfy the national pride of our former colonial masters.

Africa must unite! This was the title of one of Kwame Nkrumah's books. That call is more urgent today than ever before.

Together, we the people of Africa will be incomparably stronger internationally than we are now with our multiplicity of non-viable states. The needs of our separate countries can be, and are being, ignored by the rich and powerful. The result is that Africa is marginalised when international decisions affecting our vital interests are made.

Unity will not make us rich, but it can make it difficult for Africa and the African people to be disregarded and humiliated. And it will therefore increase the effectiveness of the decisions we make and try to implement for our development.

My generation led Africa to political freedom. The current generation of leaders and the people of Africa must pick up the flickering torch of African freedom, refuel it with their enthusiasm and determination, and carry it forward.[42]

His death was indeed a significant event in the history of Africa. It marked the end of an era in which African countries won independence, and in which the African founding fathers left an indelible mark on the young nations they helped to nurture during the post-colonial period.

In spite of the failures they had in a number of areas, especially in the economic arena, they will always be remembered as the leaders who not only led our countries to independence but who also helped end white minority rule in southern Africa by supporting liberation movements waging guerrilla warfare against the racist regimes in the region.

This concerted effort culminated in the collapse of apartheid in the citadel of white supremacy and the last bastion of white minority rule on the continent, and whose demise was witnessed by Nyerere when he attended the inauguration of Nelson Mandela as the first democratically elected president of South Africa.

The struggle for African liberation had finally come to an end. It was a struggle to which Nyerere dedicated his entire adult life. And he will always be remembered for that. Always.

Notes

1. Julius K. Nyerere, quoted by Michael T. Kaufman, "Julius Nyerere of Tanzania Dies; Preached African Socialism to the World, " in *The New York Times*, October 15, 1999, p. B1.

2. Nyerere in an interview in December 1998 with the *New Internationalist*, January-February 1999.

3. Oginga Odinga, *Not Yet Uhuru* (London: Longmans, 1967).

4. Kenneth Kaunda, *Zambia Shall Be Free* (London: Heinemann, 1962).

5. Kaunda, quoted in Colin Legum and John Drysdale, *Africa Contemporary Record: Annual Survey and Documents 1968 - 1969* (London: Africa Research Ltd., 1969), p. 250. See also *Times of Zambia*, Lusaka, Zambia, September 1968.

6. Nyerere, quoted in *Africa Contemporary Record*, ibid., p. 220.

7. Nyerere, in an address to the Tanganyika Legislative Council (LEGCO), Dar es Salaam, Tanganyika, October 22, 1959.

8. David Martin, "A Candle on Kilimanjaro," in *Southern African Features*, December 21, 2001.

9. Nelson Mandela, *Long Walk to Freedom: The Autobiography of Nelson Mandela* (New York: Little Brown & Co., 1995).

10. Yoweri Museveni, in Elizabeth Kanyogonya, editor, *Yoweri K. Museveni: What Is Africa's Problem?: Foreword by Mwalimu Julius K. Nyerere* (Minneapolis: University of Minnesota Press, 2000); Museveni, cited by Lara Santoro, "West Cheers Uganda's One-Man Show," in *The Christian Science Monitor*, March 2, 1999; Peter Graff, "Ex-Leninist Leads Uganda to Prosperity: Single-Party Rule Troubles Free-Market Admirers," in *The Boston Globe*, December 7, 1997, p. A44:

"Museveni is a guerrilla leader who spent much of his life in exile in socialist Tanzania and received his education at the University of Dar es Salaam, then a hotbed of post-colonial leftist radicalism. At the time, Tanzania's patriarch, Julius Nyerere, was a hero to most students for implementing the policy of 'ujamaa' (African socialism)... Museveni still considers himself a disciple of Nyerere."

See also Museveni, in Godfrey Mwakikagile, *Economic Development in Africa* (Commack, New York: Nova Science Publishers, Inc., 1999), p. 142.

11. Che Guevara, *Congo Diaries.*

12. P. W. Botha, in *Africa Contemporary Record*, op.cit., p. 291.

13. Walter Rodney, *How Europe Underdeveloped Africa* (Dar es Salaam, Tanzania: Tanzania Publishing House, 1972).

14. Colin Legum, "The Goal of an Egalitarian Society," in Colin Legum and Geoffrey Mmari, editors, *Mwalimu: The Influence of Nyerere* (Trenton, New Jersey: Africa World Press, 1995), p. 187.

15. Philip Ochieng', "There Was Real Freedom in Mwalimu's Day," in *The East African*, Nairobi, Kenya, October 20, 1999.

16. "In Memory of Karim Essack," the International Emergency Committee (IEC) to Defend the Life of Dr. Abimael Guzman, London, October 1997.

17. Keith B. Richburg, *Out of America: A Black Man Confronts Africa* (New York: Basic Books, 1998), p. 241. As he put it:

"One of my earliest trips was to Tanzania, and there I found a country that had actually managed to purge itself of the evil of tribalism....But after three years traveling the continent, I've found that Tanzania is the exception, not the rule."

18. Philip Ochieng', *I Accuse the Press: An Insider's View of the Media and Politics in Africa* (Initiatives Press: ACT Press).

19. Harvey Glickman, "Tanzania: From Disillusionment to Guarded Optimism," in *Current History: A Journal of Contemporary World Affairs*, May 1997, p. 217.

20. Francis Kasoma, *The Press and Multiparty Politics in Africa* (University of Tampere); F.P.Kasoma, *Communication Policies in Botswana, Lesotho, and Swaziland* (University of Tampere); F.P. Kasoma, *Communication Policies in Zambia* (Tempereen Yliopisto); F.P. Kasoma, *The Press in Zambia: The Development, Role, and Control of National Newspapers in*

Zambia 1906 - 1983 (Multimedia Publications).

21. Hadji Konde, *Press Freedom in Tanzania* (Nairobi, Kenya: Eastern Africa Publications).

22. Clement Ndulute, *The Poetry of Shaaban Robert* (Dar es Salaam, Tanzania: University of Dar es Salaam Press, 1994).

23. Godfrey Mwakikagile, *Economic Development in Africa* (Commack, New York: Nova Science Publishers, Inc., 1999).

24. Godfrey Mwakikagile, *The Modern African State: Quest for Transformation* (Huntington, New York: Nova Science Publishers, Inc., 2001).

25. Godfrey Mwakikagile, *Africa and the West* (Huntington, New York: Nova Science Publishers, Inc., 2000).

26. Godfrey Mwakikagile, book review of George B.N. Ayittey, *Africa in Chaos* (New York: St. Martin's Press, 1998), on Amazon.com, December 2001.

27. Jonathan Power, TFF Jonathan Power Columns, "Lament for Independent Africa's Greatest Leader," London, October 6, 1999.

28. Julius Nyerere, in "Julius Nyerere Press Conference," Dar es Salaam, AFP, 14 March 1995.

29. Nyerere, remarks to the World Bank, quoted in the *Sunday Times*, October 3, 1999.

30. Nyerere, in the *Sunday Independent*, Johannesburg, October 17, 1999.

31. Jomo Kenyatta, quoted in *Africa Contemporary Record*, op. cit., p. 157. See also *Kenya Weekly News*, Nairobi, Kenya, June 21, 1968:

"How will KPU contest the elections if it is not allowed to be organised on a country-wide basis like KANU?... In its brief, but turbulent history, Kenya has had numerous political parties, which in many cases died a natural death. Let KPU follow them into the grave if the Wananchi do not support its programme after a fair and full hearing of its case...." See also, same quotation, in *Africa Contemporary Record*, ibid.

32. Mundia Kamau, "A Nation in Distress," in *Mashada Daily*, Nairobi, Kenya, November 13, 1999.

33. James Mpinga, "With Mwalimu Gone, Free Bread for Butiama Children Goes Too," in *The East African*, Nairobi, Kenya, November 3, 1999.

34. "Newsweek," October 1999.

35. Ali A. Mazrui, "Nyerere and I," in *Voices*, Africa Resource Center, October 1999.

36. Jimmy Carter, on Nyerere's death, quoted in "Tanzania: Former President Julius Nyerere Dies at 77," in *UN Wire*, New York, October 15, 1999.

37. Ali A. Mazrui, "Mwalimu's Rise to Power," in *Daily Nation*, Nairobi, Kenya, October 17, 1999; "Africa's Mwalimu: Ali Mazrui Pays Tribute to Julius Nyerere," in *Worldview Magazine*, Washington, D.C., Vol. 12, No. 4, Fall 1999.

38. Ali A. Mazrui, *On Heroes and Uhuru-Worship: Essays: Independent Africa* (London: Longmans, 1967).

39. Nyerere, in an interview with James McKinley, "Tanzania's Nyerere Looks back: Many Failures, and One Big Success - Bringing A Nation to Life," in *International Herald Tribune*, September 2, 1996. See also Godfrey Mwakikagile, *Economic Development in Africa*, op. cit., p. 62. As Nyerere stated:

"I felt that these little countries in Africa were really too small, they would not be viable - the Tanganyikas, the Rwandas, the Burundis, the Kenyas. My ambition in East Africa was really never to build a Tanganyika. I wanted an East African federation. So what did I succeed in doing? My success is building a nation out of this collection of tribes."

40. Olusegun Obasanjo, at Nyerere's funeral, Dar es Salaam, Tanzania, quoted by Susan Linnee, "Tanzanian Leader's Funeral Marks End of Era," Associated Press (AP), October 22, 1999.

41. "Look Beyond Mobutu, Nyerere Tells Zaireans," in Features Africa Network, Africa Online, March 12, 1997.

42. Julius K. Nyerere, "Africa Must Unite," his speech in Accra, Ghana, March 6, 1997, marking Ghana's 40th independence anniversary; edited excerpts published by New Africa International Network (NAIN): Debate: www.nain.unitedafricastar.com/html/africa.htm. See also *Daily Graphic*, Accra, Ghana, March 1997; *Daily News*, Dar es salaam, Tanzania, March 1997.

See also Bill Sutherland and Matt Meyer, foreword by Archbishop Desmond Tutu, *Guns and Gandhi in Africa: Pan-African Insights on Nonviolence, Armed Struggle and Liberation in Africa* (Trenton, New Jersey: Africa World Press, Inc., 2000).

See also M.O. Ene, chairman, Enyimba Pan-Igbo Think Tank, on his remarks about Nyerere when he died: "I saw the legend in 1966, and the memory still lives with me."

Appendix I:

Address by Mwalimu Julius K. Nyerere, Former President of Tanzania and Chairman of the South Centre, at the Quinquennial General Conference of the Association of Commonwealth Universities. Ottawa, Canada: 17th August, 1998.

Mr. Chairman; Your Excellencies: Ladies and Gentlemen; and Friends.

You have asked me to speak on "Leadership and the Management of Change", and I have been foolhardy enough to agree. But I must make it clear that I have no theory of leadership or of management either. By profession I am a trained classroom teacher. But through an accident of history I found myself at the head of the Liberation Movement of my country, and later at the head of its Government. So I speak to you from my own experience only; it has been long, but still limited. It does not include leading a university!

Change has, throughout history, been a constant part of human experience. But today change is more rapid than ever before; its implications are very comprehensive, and yet its first approach is often imperceptible. Who in an isolated village in Africa could have foreseen the economic and social effects which would follow from the first appearance there of a tin bucket? How many people in a developing nation to-day realise that a financial collapse in a far country may affect their whole livelihood? And how many will recognise the underlying cause of the consequent changes when they do take place? For any society, and for every individual, adapting to change at the present speed is very difficult; yet avoiding change is impossible.

Decades ago, as President of my country, I told Tanzanians that the choice before them was to change or be changed. I was wrong. There was no choice. They had to change, and would still

BE changed.

In retrospect, I think that the burden of Leadership was easier for my generation than it is for the leaders of to-day. The demand for change was coming from us - the leaders and people alike. We were speaking on behalf of a united society in demanding an end to the visible, and thus easily understood, alien control over our lives.

Very few of the leaders of the Independence Movements understood that political freedom could be virtually negated by ever-increasing external economic power over us. Kwame Nkrumah of Ghana was probably the first of us to realise that fact, with his much derided talk of "neo-colonialism". But even he said "Seek ye first the political kingdom and all else will be added unto you".

The present generation of leaders have not only to deal with the effects of the economic realities about which most of us knew very little, they have also to do so when the expectations of the people are higher than the general understanding of what is happening and why. It is not easy to explain to the people why the prices they receive for their cotton, coffee, or copper seem constantly to decrease, while the prices of the things which they need to buy are always going up. How do you explain to an ordinary worker why with the same amount of money he bought more rice yesterday than he can buy to-day? And even if you could explain it, it is not explanation which the people want. They want rice at an affordable price and they want their leader to do something about it.

It was in the wilderness, on the way to the promised land of milk and honey, when the People demanded water, food, or simply a change of food, that Moses experienced the pain of being told that things were better in Egypt. When he cries to God "Lord: What shall I do with these People? In a moment they will be stoning me!" The answer was water from a rock, or manna from Heaven, or quails from somewhere. In the wilderness of globalisation and liberalisation our god or goddess is the callous and uncaring Market.

Yet leadership today is very much about water, food, jobs, shelter, education, and community. It is about organising our communities, and rallying the people to the kinds of action which will increase the supply of these goods and services to the people - all of the people. The people are not fools. When the rains fail, or El Nino causes the floods, they do not blame their government. What they do demand is that their government brings emergency food supplies, or helps them to rebuild a bridge, or do other things by which they can overcome the disaster. But they will not accept an excuse for inaction by the leaders on the plea that the IMF wants their Government to give first priority to the servicing of their country's Foreign Debt.

Organising our societies to achieve post-independence social and economic objectives was bound to be difficult even without the pressures of globalisation and the strictures of the international financial organisations.

The call for freedom from an external power unites all the victims of the system: rich and poor; educated and uneducated; Christian and Moslem; Brahman and Harijan; Hausa, Yoruba and Ibo. Everybody wants their nation to be free, and fights for it, or supports those who do.

Unfortunately however, the call to mobilise our resources so that everyone in our countries can have clean water, education, health care, and a means of earning a living, is in practice not unifying. For in almost every one of our countries there is a rich and powerful minority which is more concerned to defend their own wealth and privilege - and indeed to increase them - than it is worried about the sufferings of the poor.

Tanzania had been independent for a very short time before we began to see such a growing gap between the Haves and Have-nots of our country. We were - as we still are - a very poor country. We did not have a well-developed money-making private sector. Our privileged group was emerging from the political leaders and the bureaucrats, who had all been poor under colonial rule but were beginning to use their new positions in the Party and the Government to enrich themselves. This kind of development would alienate our leadership from the People; yet our overriding need was for the whole nation to work together to fight against what we had named as our three Enemies: POVERTY, IGNORANCE, and DISEASE.

So we articulated a new National Objective. In the Arusha Declaration of Socialism and Self-Reliance we stressed that development is about People - ALL our People, and not just a small, privileged minority. We laid down a Code of conduct for our Leaders. And we set out to try to achieve those objectives.

We had already adopted a highly sophisticated and successful democratic Single Party System. Obviously it was not based on the Westminster model, nor the US model. Nor was it based on the Kremlin model either. We did not extol it for others to follow; but it worked for us. It increased the accountability to the people of our MPs and Ministers while emphasizing the common interests and concerns of all our citizens. That was our objective.

The Arusha Declaration and our democratic single party system, together with our national language, Kiswahili, and a highly politicised and disciplined National Army, transformed what had been a motley of more than 126 different tribes into a cohesive nation. That achievement goes a long way to explain the political stability which my country still enjoys today. That stability comes under ever-increasing strain as inequalities of wealth and power within the country get greater and as our economic woes persist.

A wise Englishman once said that power corrupts and absolute power corrupts absolutely. Our single party system eventually became complacent, bureaucratic and corrupt. We had to change. We are now experimenting with a multi-party system. We have also, wrongly in my view, abandoned the Arusha Declaration. We are now experimenting with Free Market Capitalism. The rest of my remarks, therefore, are about our problems as we are trying to manage Democracy and Capitalism in to-day's international climate and imbalance of power.

In the days of the Cold War, the leading countries of the West created and supported a whole lot of corrupt dictators all over the Third World. The Marcoses, the Somozas, the Papa Docs, the Bokassas and the Mobutus of the Third World were all creatures and proteges of Western democracy. It is even said that when elections were proposed for South Vietnam the Americans opposed the idea. They feared that if the elections were free and fair the Communists would win them!

The Cold War is now over; and refreshingly the same Western Countries have now become great champions of democracy and democratic elections everywhere in the World. But now it has become their turn to preach a kind of "scientific" democracy. Democracy is being trotted out as if it is something that can be cloned like Dolly the sheep, and used anywhere and everywhere. We disagree and argue in vain that we must manage our own democratic development and change. For democracy to work properly, we argue, it must shape its mechanisms to suit the culture, the conditions and current circumstances, and also the nature and purposes of a nation and its people. That is how democracy has developed in all the Western countries. American democracy, British democracy, Canadian democracy, Swiss democracy etc. are all democracies; but they are not clones of some original prototype ? they're different. Democracies in the countries of the South should be allowed to develop their own institutions and characteristics. The people of Burundi, for instance, do not have to be apologetic about wanting to devise a democracy which suits Burundi. What is important is that it should be a democracy, but a democracy that is acceptable to the People of Burundi, and which serves their best interests.

But on top of dogmatic democracy we have now to contend with dogmatic capitalism also. Once again it is the turn of the capitalist world to insist on a kind of scientific capitalism which every country must follow. It is called: laissez-faire, free-market capitalism. Its preachers believe that it is both feasible and rational to ask Burkina Faso, and China, and India, and Russia, and Poland, and Brazil, and Tanzania, and Laos and Fiji to clone American capitalism. But once again this is absurd. Do we really have one capitalism in the capitalist world of to-day? Are German capitalism, French capitalism, Italian capitalism, Japanese capitalism, Korean capitalism all clones of American and British capitalism? Have they developed in the same way? The answer is clearly no. For once again in real life no country operates a pure laissez-faire capitalism. Why then, are capitalists of the South not being allowed to develop their own forms of capitalism?

Mr Chairman: this Association of Commonwealth Universities is, like all Commonwealth associations, a consultative body. It enables members to share their problems and to discuss possible ways of managing them It promotes and facilitates schemes of co-operation or mutual help among all, or any group of, its members. But the ACU exercises no authority over them and no power has been delegated to it. And although you learn from one another, no university is trying to turn all the others into clones of itself. Your inequalities of resources and experience are known but merged into mutual respect. The ACU promotes the separate uniqueness as well as the equality of all members.

There are something approaching 200 sovereign nation states in the world, and even more economic and social units. Each of them is in some way different from all the others. But unavoidably they affect each other. So international organisations and functional institutions have been created. Some of these international bodies do necessarily have executive functions, and thus have delegated power.

Unfortunately, those international institutions which do have executive power have all been established in a manner which increases rather than decreases the relative POWER in the world of the already most powerful nations and economic units. This is especially true as regards organisations concerned with finance and trade, where voting on the governing boards is based on the wealth and trade of members.

Thus, these theoretically independent and objective functional institutions are, in reality, controlled by a cabal of the wealthiest, the most developed, and the most assertive national governments of the world. The I.M.F., the World Trade Organisation, and the World Bank, have become a smokescreen under the cover of which the major developed nations use their immense economic power in their own exclusive interests.

There was a time when a developing country leader could say "No" to the IMF or World Bank. But no leader of a highly indebted poor country, or a financially troubled Indonesia or South Korea, can with impunity say "No" today. His country will be crucified! So a time comes when the leader is forced to accept a neo-colonial status for his country in return for a financial bailout from its international creditors. This is the case today in many African countries.

As strong states have become less inclined to risk the lives of their soldiers in overseas adventures, it is now mostly economic power which they use to secure their own interests and international purposes. That pressure is often explained to their own people in the name of supporting human rights and democracy. Good people often support such pressure on those grounds. They do not realise that abuses of fundamental human rights are - not infrequently - the direct result of South leaders trying to maintain political stability while they force IMF medicine down the throats of their people! The result may be what are called "IMF bread riots". If these are put down by force or by political sleight of hand, the dissatisfaction of the people may fester and break out later into general social unrest or even civil war.

But leadership cannot be about telling people what to do and then (if they don't like it) forcing them to do it by the use of the Police or the Military. And in any case to use force against hungry people who are protesting against an increase in their poverty should be considered obscene by any modern society.

Indonesia had for years been quoted to African developing countries as an example of "how to develop". We were urged to copy it. In vain we pointed to the different circumstances of the African and South-East Asian countries; in vain we pointed out that none of the so-called "Asian Tigers" had developed through following laissez-faire capitalist theory.

Yet now that Indonesia has become the victim of international currency speculation and its President has been forced to resign, we are hearing the usual explanations for its failure: it was a corrupt and dictatorial state which denied human rights to its people, and which stifled their initiative by smothering their freedom. It is now quoted to us as an awful warning rather than an example!

The relentless and single-minded drive by the rich and powerful to globalise and liberalise; to privatise every public enterprise; to deify the Market; to weaken our governments and make it impossible for them to intervene decisively on behalf of the poor and powerless: all this will, no doubt, succeed in creating immense wealth and power for a minority of countries and a minority of citizens in every country. But it is also creating massive poverty and hopelessness for the majority of the countries of the world and their citizens.

This cannot be a good recipe for peace and security in the world; for genuine peace and security within nations and between nations is a result of justice. If peace in the world is to become a possibility, the governance of international institutions must be based on some kind of appropriate democracy - on some basis of accountability to the people of the world. As the world becomes increasingly one, its governance should become increasingly democratic and just. It is not moving in that direction. On the contrary, governance at the international level, when it is not simply chaotic is becoming increasingly arrogant, authoritarian and

unjust. A nation so governed cannot have peace and stability. Nor does it deserve to have peace and stability. A world so governed cannot be an exception.

    Thank you.

Appendix II:

An Interview with Nyerere

New Internationalist, December 1998

The first issue of *The Internationalist* in (October) 1970 had as its cover story an interview with President Julius Nyerere of Tanzania, then at the very centre of the new movement for world development.

Mwalimu Julius Nyerere

Three decades on, Nyerere is, Mandela aside, Africa's most respected elder statesperson, still active in attempts to resolve the current conflicts in Burundi and DR Congo. No-one is better placed to look back on the anti-colonial century. Ikaweba Bunting interviewed him for the *New Internationalist*.

The briefings and consultations at the Burundi peace negotiations in Arusha, Tanzania, had been going on all day. It was now seven in the evening and we had been at it non-stop for more than 12 hours. This was a tedious and demanding task, listening to each party go through their interpretation of history and presenting their case. There was a lot of repetition, political manoeuvring and tension. Patience was a most valuable asset.

I was beginning to feel the enormity of the task coupled with the strain of such an intense process - and all I had been doing was taking notes. So I knew that a 76-year-old man in the eye of the storm had to be exhausted. But he showed no sign of it.

The old man, Mwalimu Julius Nyerere - former President of Tanzania and one of Africa's most revered twentieth-century leaders - had been asked by the Organization of African Unity (in 1998) to act as Facilitator, getting the warring parties in Burundi to negotiate a political settlement. I remember that he had a studied reluctance before accepting the task. But since he undertook the work he has never shown a trace of doubt that a negotiated and equitable peace would be achieved. And, as the conflict in the Democratic Republic of the Congo (DRC) evolves, overtures are being made to involve him in seeking a political solution - he is felt to be the only person who could talk to all sides involved in the conflict and to whom they might all listen.

Now, at the end of this exhausting day, a discussion began on the current war in the DRC. Mwalimu became animated. He began to elaborate on the political implications of the wars in the Great Lakes region of Central Africa.

He was very disturbed by the growing belligerence of the countries involved and the increase in mass murders. He expressed particular concern about the persecution of the Batutsi based on the mythical racial theory that categorizes them as Hamitic, Caucasian black people who must be exterminated because of their sinister plans to rule Africa. He said he felt a tinge of embarrassment because he had boasted only months earlier that Africa was entering a new era and managing its own problems. "Now the stupidity of fighting over this big forest is going to set us back. Mobutu always gave us problems but we never fought over the Congo."

Some of the senior members of the team begged their leave but I stayed, soaking up as much as I could, aware that moments like these are jewels to be treasured. Finally he exclaimed: "We are going to have to think about this some more and consider what can be done to stop this awful killing and get some kind of peace in our region." I could tell by his tone and body language that this meant 'good night'. As I was leaving, Mwalimu - the word means 'teacher' and has been Nyerere's respectful title among Tanzanians for decades - called me back to say: "You have to get your Pan-African Working Group together and start tackling this problem; let's arrange another meeting."

It has been my privilege to be associated with Mwalimu Nyerere for the past 25 years. During a visit to Harlem, New York, in the late 1960s Mwalimu extended an invitation to Africans in the Diaspora to come to Tanzania and participate in building a socialist African state. I came over through a new organization called the Pan-African Skills project and have lived in Tanzania ever since, for a quarter of the century.

Nyerere's Tanzania was a magnet then for anti-colonial activists and thinkers from all over the world. Uganda's President Yoweri Museveni, for instance, was deeply influenced by his time as a student at the University of Dar-es-Salaam. Museveni belonged to a study group led by the Guyanan Walter Rodney, who wrote his seminal book *How Europe Underdeveloped Africa* while he was a professor there.

The University of Dar-es-Salaam became the centre for the guerrilla-intellectuals and activists of African liberation movements. FRELIMO of Mozambique, the ANC and PAC of South Africa, ZANU and ZAPU of Zimbabwe, the MPLA of Angola and SWAPO of Namibia all had offices and training camps in Tanzania. The country also gave safe haven to US civil-rights activists, Black Panther party-members and Vietnam War resisters.

It was an exciting place to be. Under a head of state who valued equal rights, justice and development more than the pomp and power of office, Tanzania was at the heart of the anti-colonial struggle.

Over the years I have often been able to sit with Mwalimu and reflect on Africa's struggles for self-determination and development. Now, in December 1998, prompted by the *New Internationalist* special issue on The Radical Twentieth Century, Mwalimu Nyerere and I sat down over two days at his home in Butiama, Tanzania, and reflected on his role over the past 50 years as an activist and statesperson in the anti-colonial cause.

What was the anti-colonial movement's greatest contribution to humanity?

There are two fundamental things that the anti-colonial liberation movement contributed to humanity. The first is simply that the suffering of a whole chunk of human beings through the actions of others was halted. The arrogance of one group of people in lording it over the human race and exploiting the poorer peoples was challenged and discredited - and that was a positive contribution made by the liberation struggle to all humanity.

Second, the liberation movement was very moral. It was not simply liberation in a vacuum. Gandhi argued a moral case and so did I. Liberation freed white people also. Take South Africa: there, the anti-apartheid victory freed whites as well as black people.

When did you first encounter the idea of liberation from colonialism?

I cannot say I encountered the idea of liberation in a totality like a flash of light. I did not have an experience like Paul on the road to Damascus. For me it was a process - something that grew inside of me. Our elders fought and were defeated by the Germans and the British. We were born under colonialism. Some of us never questioned it. Those who got educated began to think about it. What many of us went through was simply a desire to be accepted by the white man. At first this is what it was - a kind of inert dissatisfaction that we were not accepted as equals.

World War Two and what it was fought for - democracy and freedom - started the process for many people, especially those who were in the Army. For me the transformation came later. At Makerere in 1943 I started something called the Tanganyika African Welfare Association. Its main purpose was not political or anti-colonial. We wanted to improve the lives of Africans. But inside us something was happening.

I wrote an essay in 1944 called "The Freedom of Women." I must be honest and say I was influenced by John Stuart Mill, who had written about the subjugation of women. My father had 22 wives and I knew how hard they had to work and what they went through as women. Here in this essay I was moving towards the idea of freedom theoretically. But I was still in the mindset of improving the lives and welfare of Africans: I went to Tabora to start teaching.

Then came Indian independence. The significance of India's independence movement was that it shook the British Empire. When Gandhi succeeded I think it made the British lose the will to cling to empire. But it was events in Ghana in 1949 that fundamentally changed my attitude. When Kwame Nkrumah was released from prison this produced a transformation. I was in Britain and oh you could see it in the Ghanaians! They became different human beings, different from all the rest of us! This thing of freedom began growing inside all of us. First India in 1947, then Ghana in 1949. Ghana became independent eight years later. Under the influence of these events, while at university in Britain, I made up my mind to be a full-time political activist when I went back home. I intended to work for three years and then launch into politics. But it happened sooner than I planned.

Independence came in 1961, and Nyerere became president. Six years later, he issued the Arusha Declaration, which nailed Tanzania's colours firmly to the mast of socialism and self-reliance. The great Caribbean historian CLR James once called the Arusha Declaration 'the highest stage of resistance ever reached by revolting Blacks.'

Does the Arusha Declaration still stand up today?

I still travel around with it. I read it over and over to see what I would change. Maybe I would improve on the Kiswahili that was used but the Declaration is still valid: I would not change a thing. Tanzania had been independent for a short time before we began to see a growing gap between the haves and the have-nots in our country. A privileged group was emerging from the political leaders and bureaucrats who had been poor under colonial rule but were now beginning to use their positions in the Party and the Government to enrich themselves. This kind of development would alienate the leadership from the people. So we articulated a new national objective: we stressed that development is about all our people and not just a small and privileged minority.

The Arusha Declaration was what made Tanzania distinctly Tanzania. We stated what we stood for, we laid down a code of conduct for our leaders and we made an effort to achieve our goals. This was obvious to all, even if we made mistakes - and when one tries anything new and uncharted there are bound to be mistakes.

The Arusha Declaration and our democratic single-party system, together with our national language, Kiswahili, and a highly politicized and disciplined national army, transformed more than 126 different tribes into a cohesive and stable nation.

However, despite this achievement, they say we failed in Tanzania, that we floundered. But did we? We must say no. We can't deny everything we accomplished. There are some of my friends whom we did not allow to get rich; now they are getting rich and they say 'See, we are getting rich now, so you were wrong'. But what kind of answer is that?

The floundering of socialism has been global. This is what needs an explanation, not just the Tanzanian part of it. George Bernard Shaw, who was an atheist, said, 'You cannot say Christianity has failed because it has never been tried.' It is the same with socialism: you cannot say it has failed because it has never been tried.

After independence you pursued an African socialism while in Kenya Jomo Kenyatta embraced a more conservative nationalism. The two of you came to symbolize opposing visions of development. Were you conscious at the time of the need to chart a different course that might inspire other new African nations?

Anti-colonialism was a nationalist movement. For me liberation and unity were the most important things. I have always said that I was African first and socialist second. I would rather see a free and united Africa before a fragmented socialist Africa. I did not preach socialism. I made this distinction deliberately so as not to divide the country. The majority in the anti-colonial struggle were nationalist. There was a minority who argued that class was the central issue, that white workers were as exploited as black workers by capitalism. They wanted to approach liberation in purely Marxist terms. However, in South Africa white workers oppressed black workers. It was more than class and I saw that.

Jomo Kenyatta was clearly capitalist and we were trying a different course. But I must confess I did not see myself as charting out something for the rest of Africa. One picks one's way. I never saw the contradictions that would prevent Kenya, Uganda and Tanzania from working together. I was naïve, I guess. Even now for me freedom and unity are paramount.

I respected Jomo (Kenyatta) immensely. It has probably never happened before in history. Two heads of state, Milton Obote [Uganda's leader] and I, went to Jomo and said to him: 'let's unite our countries and you be our head of state'. He said no. I think he said no because it would have put him out of his element as a Kikuyu Elder.

In 1990 you were quoted as saying that you thought the absence of an opposition party had contributed to the Tanzanian ruling party's abandonment of its commitments. Do you think it was a mistake for so many new African nations to opt for a one-party state?

I never advocated this for everyone. But I did for Tanzania because of our circumstances then. In 1990 the Chama Cha Mapinduzi (CCM) abandoned the one-party state for a multi-party system. But we do not have an opposition. The point I was making when I made the statement was that any party that stays in power too long becomes corrupt. The Communist Party in the Soviet Union, the CCM of Tanzania and the Conservative Party of Britain all stayed in power too long and became corrupt. This is especially so if the opposition is too weak or non-existent.

What were your main mistakes as Tanzanian leader? What should you have done differently?

There are things that I would have done more firmly or not at all. For example, I would not nationalize the sisal plantations. This was a mistake. I did not realize how difficult it would be for the state to manage agriculture. Agriculture is difficult to socialize. I tried to tell my government that what was traditionally the family's in the village social organization should be left with the family, while what was new could be communalized at the village level. The land issue and family holdings were very sensitive. I saw this intellectually but it was hard to translate it into policy implementation. But I still think that in the end Tanzania will return to the values and basic principles of the Arusha Declaration.

Why did your attempt to find a new way founder on the rocks?

I was in Washington last year (1997). At the World Bank the first question they asked me was 'how did you fail?' I responded that we took over a country with 85 per cent of its adult population illiterate. The British ruled us for 43 years. When they left, there were 2 trained engineers and 12 doctors. This is the country we inherited.

When I stepped down there was 91-per-cent literacy and nearly every child was in school. We trained thousands of engineers and doctors and teachers.

In 1988 Tanzania's per-capita income was $280. Now, in 1998, it is $140. So I asked the World Bank people what went wrong. Because for the last ten years Tanzania has been signing on the dotted line and doing everything the IMF and the World Bank wanted. Enrolment in school has plummeted to 63 per cent and conditions in health and other social services have deteriorated. I asked them again: 'what went wrong?' These people just sat there looking at me. Then they asked what could they do? I told them have some humility. Humility - they are so arrogant!

Do you think Third World independence actually suited the industrialized world, leaving it with the economic power but without the political responsibility?

It seems that independence of the former colonies has suited the interests of the industrial world for bigger profits at less cost. Independence made it cheaper for them to exploit us. We became neo-colonies. Some African leaders did not realize it. In fact many argued against Kwame (Nkrumah)'s idea of neo-colonialism.

The majority of countries in Africa and the rest of the South are hamstrung by debt, by the IMF. We have too much debt now. It is a heavy burden, a trap. It is debilitating. We must have a new chance. If we doubled our production and debt-servicing capabilities we would still have no money for anything extra like education or development. It is immoral. It is an affront. The conditions and policies of the World Bank and the IMF are to enable countries to pay debt not to develop. That is all! Let us argue the moral case. Let us create a new liberation movement to free us from immoral debt and neo-colonialism. This is one way forward. The other way is through Pan-African unity.

Should African resistance movements have embraced Pan-Africanism more readily? Do you think we should be working now towards a federal United States of Africa?

Kwame Nkrumah and I were committed to the idea of unity. African leaders and heads of state did not take Kwame seriously. However, I did. I did not believe in these small little nations. Still today I do not believe in them. I tell our people to look at the European Union, at these people who ruled us who are now uniting.

Kwame and I met in 1963 and discussed African Unity. We differed on how to achieve a United States of Africa. But we both agreed on a United States of Africa as necessary. Kwame went to Lincoln University, a black college in the US. He perceived things from the perspective of US history, where the 13 colonies that revolted against the British formed a union. That is what he thought the OAU should do.

I tried to get East Africa to unite before independence. When we failed in this I was wary about Kwame's continental approach. We corresponded profusely on this. Kwame said my idea of 'regionalization' was only balkanization on a larger scale. Later African historians will have to study our correspondence on this issue of uniting Africa.

Africans who studied in the US like Nkrumah and [Nigerian independence leader] Azikiwe were more aware of the Diaspora and the global African community than those of us who studied in Britain. They were therefore aware of a wider Pan-Africanism. Theirs was the aggressive Pan-Africanism of WEB Dubois and Marcus Garvey. The colonialists were against this and frightened of it.

After independence the wider African community became clear to me. I was concerned about education; the work of Booker T Washington resonated with me. There were skills we needed and black people outside Africa had them. I gave our US Ambassador the specific job of recruiting skilled Africans from the US Diaspora. A few came, like you. Some stayed; others left.

We should try to revive it. We should look to our brothers and sisters in the West. We should build the broader Pan-Africanism. There is still the room - and the need.

******

Timeline on Nyerere

1922 Julius Nyerere is born in Butiama, near Lake Victoria, son of a chief of the Zanaki, one of Tanzania's and Africa's smallest ethnic groups.

1943 Nyerere launches the Tanganyika African Welfare Association while at Makerere University in Uganda.

1949 Goes to study history and economics at Edinburgh University in Scotland; first Tanganyikan at a British university.

1952 Returns home to Tanganyika and becomes a teacher or mwalimu.

1954 Launches the Tanganyika African National Union (TANU).

1955 Visits UN headquarters in New York to press for independence.

1960 Finally agrees on terms with Britain and becomes chief minister of the British colony of Tanganyika.

1961 Becomes first prime minister of an independent Tanganyika. He promotes Kiswahili as a national language and emphasizes literacy and education. He also gives unconditional support to liberation movements in neighbouring countries such as FRELIMO in Mozambique.

1962 On the country's first independence anniversary, Tanganyika becomes a republic and Nyerere president.

1963 Nyerere is a prime mover in the creation of the Organization of African Unity (OAU).

1964 Zanzibar unites with Tanganyika to become the Republic of Tanzania, with Nyerere as president.

1965 Tanzania officially becomes a one-party state under the leadership of Nyerere.

1967 The Arusha Declaration lays out Tanzania's commitment to socialism and self-reliance. It gives priority to agriculture under a form of communal land ownership traditionally known in Kiswahili as ujamaa (literally 'familyhood').

1977 Nyerere's ruling party (TANU on mainland Tanzania) merges with Zanzibar's Afro-Shirazi Party to become Chama Cha Mapinduzi (CCM), a Kiswahili name which means the Party of the Revolution or Revolutionary Party. The East African Community (EAC) of Tanzania, Kenya and Uganda collapses in the same year.

1978 Tanzania is invaded by troops of the Ugandan dictator Idi Amin and responds by giving military help to the Ugandan resistance movement that eventually kicks him out of power with the help of Tanzanian troops.

1979 Idi Amin is ousted from power and flees the country after Tanzania launches a counter-offensive and Tanzanian troops and an army of Ugandan exiles based in Tanzania cross the border into Uganda and march all the way to the Ugandan capital Kampala.

1985 Nyerere retires as president, handing over to Ali Hassan Mwinyi.

1986 Nyerere becomes head of the South-South Commission in Geneva which aims to strengthen Third World unity.

1996 The Mwalimu Nyerere Foundation is established in Dar-es-Salaam, working to promote peace, unity and people-centred development throughout Africa and the world.

1998 Nyerere is asked by the OAU to act as facilitator trying to resolve the conflict in Burundi between the Hutu and the Tutsi.

1999 Nyerere dies, marking the end of an era.

******

Nyerere died almost a year later, on October 14, 1999, after this interview was conducted by Ikaweba Bunting for the *New Internationalist*. In November 2002, the first edition of my book, *Nyerere and Africa: End of an Era*, was published. An expanded edition was published in January 2005. - Godfrey Mwakikagile.

Appendix III:

Obote Remembers Nyerere

Former Ugandan president, Dr. Milton Obote, was interviewed by Andrew Mwenda of the Ugandan *Monitor* in Lusaka, Zambia, in October 2004. Obote died in the same month a year later.

Fighting Idi Amin: 1971-79

Having raised 900 volunteers to resist the military coup by Idi Amin, we took the recruits to Owiny Kibul in southern Sudan for training. We had been given permission by Gen. Jaffer Nimeiri, the president of Sudan, to use his country's territory to train an army and launch an attack against Amin from Northern Uganda.

We expanded Owiny Kibul with farms and modern housing. After significant progress in our plans for an invasion, President Nimeiri entered an agreement with the Anyanya rebels led by Joseph Lagu to stop hostilities. Emperor Haile Selassie of Ethiopia had mediated the talks.

I must say that during my stay in Khartoum, President Nimeiri treated me very well. Whenever I wanted to see him, I would call state house or president's office in Khartoum and if he was in the country, I would meet GeneralNimeiri that same day or the next day. Whenever I went to see him, Nimeiri was always very kind, generous and understanding of our cause. I consider him to be a true African nationalist.

After the agreement, I was saddened when Nimeiri called me

and told me that we could not stay in Owiny Kibul, because Anyanya wanted it to be their headquarters for implementation of the agreement. I reported this to President Julius Nyerere of Tanzania.

Then Nyerere sent a delegate to Nimeiri and it was decided that our recruits be transferred to Port Sudan to be taken by ship to Tanga in Tanzania.

We moved the recruits by road to Khartoum en-route to Port Sudan. I met them at an army barracks outside Khartoum and addressed them.

I left for Dar-es-Salaam by air and was received at the airport by President Nyerere. This time he did not take me to State House but to Musasani, a suburb in Dar-es-Salaam where Nyerere used to stay. He took me to a house only two blocks away from his, and that is where I found Mama Miria and the children. I had not seen my family since I left for Singapore and it was an ecstatic moment to see them again.

I had no hand in getting Mama and the children out of Uganda. I had heard that they were arrested and Amin nearly killed the children. I had been living in Khartoum from March 1971 to July 1972.

Back to our recruits, the men arrived in Tanga but they were very sick. The ship was contaminated with a disease called meningitis, many people died on the ship and they were buried at sea.

When they arrived in Tanga, I went to see them, I found them very sick but Tanzanian medical service did a wonderful job. In three weeks people who were very sick were now healthy.

I went again and asked them to do what they did in Owiny Kibul: start farming and build good houses, which they begun immediately.

A few days later, I got a shocker from President Nyerere and his security people. Nyerere came with his intelligence staff and they told me that a one Yoweri Museveni, who has been a student at Dar-es-Salaam and had later worked in my office as a research assistant had informed them that he had organised armies in Western Uganda, in Masaka and in Jinja and Mbale.

This was not the first time I heard about Museveni. I had in fact heard about him before... even before I left for Khartoum in

March 1971. Someone had told me that someone called Museveni had arrived and had gone to Morogoro where Tanzania had given us a camp for those Ugandans who wanted to be trained as guerrillas. I did not think much about him. Now it was 1972.

When Nyerere told me about Museveni and his troops in Mbarara, Masaka, Jinja and Mbale, I said, "Can you give me time Mr. President to check?" he agreed and said, "Take your time." I started working the telephones to people in Mbarara, Masaka, Kampala, Jinja and Mbale. I regret to say that I found no trace of recruitment and I reported this to Nyerere advising him that we should not trust that story. But Nyerere believed it because it was from his intelligence service. He trusted his intelligence very much.

Within a short time, Nyerere asked me to make preparations for invasion of Uganda. Amin had dreamt to expel Asians on the 17th September. I had a meeting with Nyerere and we calculated that the invasion should coincide with the expulsion of the Asians. I felt that the expulsion of the Asians may be popular with a few people but not the majority of Ugandans.

We started preparing for the attack. I went with Vice President Rashid Kawawa several times to the camp to prepare the recruits for the attack. But moving 700 men from Tanga to Mutukula became very difficult.

Anyhow, when they arrived at Tabora, in the middle of Tanzania, there was another group of people who had been to Morogoro to be added onto the 700 recruits.

The Morogoro people were not trained at all whereas the Tanga people had been thoroughly trained in Owiny Kibul. We moved them to Mutukula.

There were two segments to the planning: one group was to fly from Arusha to Entebbe and was commanded by Oyite Ojok. This group would capture the airport, and drive towards Kampala. They would find a contingent of troops from within Uganda's army with tanks along Entebbe Road.

Their combined armoured force would then march and capture Kampala and Oyite Ojok would make an announcement of Amin's fall and play a tape with a speech I had recorded. Tragedy befell this group when the tyres of the DC10 East African Airways aircraft burst while the plane was landing at Arusha.

Another group was to enter Masaka and Mbarara through Mutukula commanded by Tito Okello. It was to be an infantry invasion. Once it had entered Uganda, it was supposed to be joined by Museveni's army along the road to Masaka and Mbarara towns.

Museveni had told Nyerere he had trained an army in these areas which would be waiting to join and support the forces from Tanzania. If all this materialised, Nyerere had promised to send in Tanzanian troops to support our land invasion.

Everything went as planned on the infantry invasion, except for the usual problems of delayed take-off, bad roads and so on and so forth. However, when our troops advanced unto Masaka town, there were no Museveni troops.

The same applied when the troops advanced on Mbarara town. On Mbarara side, only one person, the husband of Frank Mwine's sister joined our troops. Museveni had lied!!

Whether Museveni had any troops at all, we never saw any. So, Masaka was a failure, Mbarara was a failure. Our troops fought gallantly but against heavy odds and were beaten. Many including Alex Ojera, Picho Ali and Capt. Oyile were captured and later executed by Amin.

Amin's army then went from House to house and picked up our leaders and killed them. Among those killed was Bananuka together with his three sons.

Later, I was told that the man whom our troops picked before Mbarara Town who was supposed to be part of Museveni's imaginary army, was the one who went house to house and made Idi Amin's people pick up people like Bananuka.

I do not have first class evidence, but this was what my informants told me.

Later, I met Museveni casually after the invasion was crushed. He was preparing to go to Moshi to be a teacher. I developed a very low opinion of him because I now knew him to be a liar.

My contempt for Museveni is based on my personal convictions as an individual shaped by my upbringing at home, and also on my institutional socialisation as a leader. I felt then, and still feel so now, that Museveni is a dangerous man.

First, to deceive an African government and its president that was risking everything to help us liberate our country from tyranny, that he had organised troops when he did not was a very bad and dishonourable act by him.

Two, to deceive us, his colleagues, who were prepared to fight the same cause with him that he had an army yet he did not have anything showed a callous mind that just wanted to kill people.

We were not prepared to send troops to Uganda if we had known that Museveni had no troops.

When the invasion was crushed, I asked Nyerere to give me a piece of land. He gave me a piece of land in Tabora district and I organised a very big farm of Ugandan exiles, of former guerrillas. And they became very rich through farming. Between September 1972 and 1978, we did not have much activity.

I felt that if I left our troops redundant, they would forget why they were in Tanzania. So I organised some of the men who were recruited from Sudan who were carpenters to be in Mwanza and to make boats so they could pretend to be fishing but spy on Uganda.

And by the time Amin attacked Tanzania in 1978, our boats were going as far as Masaka, as far as Busia to the east.

There were some incidents in Dar Es Salaam which are worth noting.

Sometime in the 1970s, Princess Elizabeth Bagaya of Toro arrived to celebrate Saba Saba Day (July 7th) in Dar-es-Salaam. She was Amin's foreign minister and I sat next to her, with Nyerere to my right and Kenneth Kaunda next to Nyerere.

Bagaya asked me to return to Uganda, saying that home was very quiet. She said Uganda was now a stable and peaceful country. I said, "My dear sister, I am inviting you to join us in exile. Amin is not a man to be trusted. This is an opportunity for you to run away before he kills you." Bagaya simply waved me to silence.

Few months later I heard that Amin had accused Bagaya of sleeping with white people in a lavatory at an airport in Europe.

Bagaya's story is sad because I had predicted Amin just right: he began looking for her to kill her but fortunately she escaped to Kenya.

When I heard that Bagaya was staying with Dr. Mungai in Nairobi, I phoned Dr. Mungai's home and I talked to Bagaya.

In retrospect, I think I was unfair to her because after

exchanging greetings, I immediately said to her: "Didn't I tell you?" She said, "Ah, Dr. Obote, don't say that 'I told you so,' it does not help anybody." Later, I realised that that was too hard on her. I knew Bagaya very well. I had met her during the 1961-1962 London conferences.

Bagaya's father, King George Rukidi III of Toro was very a close personal friend and he introduced Bagaya to me. Rukidi had a son in the foreign office called Steven Karamagi whom he wanted to be his heir, but Bagaya wanted her own brother David Olimi Kaboyo instead.

I knew of this because the king told me and also because Bagaya used to tell us with Godfrey Binaisa.

In November 1978, I was in Lusaka where I had come to visit my friend President Kenneth Kaunda and I was staying at State House. Then I heard on BBC that Amin had attacked Kagera region in Northern Tanzania and annexed it to Uganda.

Immediately after that, Nyerere rang me. "Milton," Nyerere said with excitement in his voice, "this is what we have been waiting for. Please come back." I said, "I am a guest here, I cannot just leave." Then Nyerere said, "I have spoken to Kenneth and he is going to arrange for you to come back." However, it took about a week before President Kaunda found an aircraft for me.

Meanwhile, Nyerere was ringing every day asking me to go to Dar-es-Salaam and Kaunda was failing to get us an aircraft. The day he got an aircraft for us to go, the Rhodesian army started bombing the airport at Lusaka. It was a very strange thing indeed because again we did not leave that day. We left the next day.

Immediately I arrived in Dar-es-Salaam, I went directly to my house in Musasani and Nyerere arrived a few minutes later. We were happy to meet again. We immediately began to discuss plans for an offensive against Amin.

Nyerere asked me to mobilise the Ugandans we had trained in Tanzania, and also raise more recruits inside Uganda. He also told me that "now we are going to fight Amin until we reach Entebbe and Kampala." I said "I will try." There was a mood of excitement. I started ringing everybody in Kampala, Fort Portal, Mbarara, anybody whose telephone number I could find, I rang and asked to send more men.

The UPC was very popular, because a lot of men were sent. I raised about 900 recruits. I went to the camp of the recruits we already had in Tabora and talked to the men and said now, our patience has paid off. Tanzania now wants us to get ready. Get into your companies and platoons and get into training quickly.

Then something happened; there was a group in Nairobi led by Robert Serumaga involved with a few other people and they got in touch. I think Museveni knew about them, because they got in touch with Tanzanian security which was close to Museveni.

They came to Tanzania, went to Tabora, were allowed to address the men in the training camp. They took 300 recruits to Musoma claiming that they were going to Jinja to attack.

Apparently, Museveni had claimed that he had an army in Jinja waiting to be supported. I did not know about that. In any case, I had lost trust in Museveni and his claims to having an army. The men were put onto two boats to go to Jinja. The first boat was big and collapsed in the middle of Kagera channel and people began drowning. A smaller one was behind, people were crying, very few people were saved.

After returning from Lusaka, Nyerere had given me the task of bringing more recruits. He had also given me another task, to write papers on organising a conference, which I started drafting, and presenting to him through his intelligence service.

After I had done that I received an invitation from the organisers to go to a conference of Ugandan exiles in Moshi to discuss a post Amin Uganda.

I was happy about the invitation, which came to me through the director of intelligence. I accepted to attend, again through him.

Then Nyerere came to see me and said "Milton don't go. These people have done nothing. You are not of the same status as these people meeting in Moshi." Later, he wrote me a very beautiful letter with quotations from Shakespeare.

Unfortunately I have lost that letter. I hope someone who reads this article and has that letter can send it to me because it has fond memories.

Nyerere did not tell me the actual reason for stopping me from going to Moshi.

The reason he gave me above was unconvincing and to be

honest, I was not happy. However, in respect to him as a great leader, and to our friendship and comradeship, I accepted his decision.

Later, I learnt the actual reasons and understood why Nyerere stopped me. With hindsight, I could see how painful this must have been on him. Apparently, the British government was very scared of me returning as president.

They wanted Yusuf Lule to succeed Amin. The British felt that if I personally attended the conference, I would overshadow Lule.

The organisers, the Gang of Four were so scared of me that they even stopped Tito Okello, the commander of the Uganda liberation force, Kikosi Mwalum, from going to Moshi. Tito Okello was taken to Moshi by Olara Otunu.

Olara Otunu came with Godfrey Binaisa from America only to find that Tito Okello, his uncle, was not in the conference.

When Olara Otunu came to see me in Dar-es-Salaam, I briefed him why Tito Okello was not in the conference. The Gang of Four - Nabudere, Omwony Ojok, Edward Rugumayo and Yash Tandon, stopped Tito Okello, Chris Rwakasisi, Samwiri Mugwisa and many UPC people from attending the conference.

Even Paul Muwanga had been blocked until Olara Otunu said those people who are leading at the frontline should be at the conference. That is how Tito Okello and Muwanga were allowed to attend.

Meantime, I met Museveni again just before the Moshi conference. He came back from the front and met me on his way to Moshi.

He suggested to me that we form a joint front of the fighting forces between Kikosi Mwalumu, which was under Tito Okello and David Oyite Ojok, and his Front for National Salvation (FRONASA) on a fifty-fifty percent basis.

I did not think he had troops worth anything, and besides, the idea was to form a united political, not military front. He said he did not want to go to Moshi and find people who have contributed nothing to the liberation struggle to be pretending to organise a national front. He wanted us to have a front of those who had fighting forces on the ground.

Then Museveni asked me to form a military front with him against the Gang of Four. I told him that Nyerere had stopped me from attending the conference at Moshi. He asked me rhetorically, "Nyerere stopped you? Why?" I said, "Well, you go and ask him."

How Lule became president

How did Lule come about? When I returned from seeing the boat people who had survived the tragedy to Jinja, I found Lule in Dar Es Salaam. I said, "Oh Professor, have you come to join us?" He said, "No, no, I am a sick man, I have just come to acquaint myself with what was going on." I did not believe him because I had heard about the British who had supplied arms to the Tanzania to cross Kagera on condition that Obote does not replace Amin.

This plot to force Lule on the people of Uganda was so poorly executed at Moshi so that when the conference was delayed by one day from opening, the BBC and all the British press reported the Lule had been elected leader of Ugandan exiles in Tanzania - clearly showing that information about the manipulation of the vote had been leaked to the British.

In Moshi itself, there was a lot of haggling over who should lead the front.

At one time, delegates walked out protesting the undemocratic manner in which the organisers were conducting the conference and it took a lot of compromise to bring them back in.

Lule's nomination was bitterly opposed and UPC delegates supported Paulo Muwanga.

It is Tito Okello who suggested a compromise that Lule should become chairman of the National Executive Council and Muwanga, the chairman of the Military Commission.

That is how Lule became president of Uganda, with only a handful of votes from Ugandan exiles in Tanzania and only in the context where the organisers blocked many Ugandans from attending.

Appendix IV:

Mwalimu Julius Nyerere: An Intellectual in Power

First Mwalimu Nyerere Memorial Lecture, in Commemoration of the 6th Anniversary of Mwalimu Julius Nyerere's death, organised by the East African Students Society, University of Cape Town, South Africa,12 October 2005.

Professor Haroub Othman, Institute of Development Studies, University of Dar es Salaam, Tanzania

I want first of all to thank the East African Students Society, and the University of Cape Town in general, for organising this occasion to commemorate the death of Mwalimu Julius Nyerere; and for inviting me to give this lecture on someone I very much respect and admire.

In my life I have met many African leaders, and if I could mention a few, and in order not to cause offence, only dead ones: Kwame Nkrumah of Ghana, Ahmed Sekou Toure of Guinea, Ferhat Abbas of Algeria, Augustinho Neto of Angola, Samora Machel of Mozambique, Amilcar Cabral of Guinea Bissau and Cape Verde, and Oginga Odinga of Kenya.

I have also met several South African leaders, including historic personalities such as Oliver Tambo, Yusuf Daddoo,

Walter Sisulu, Govan Mbeki, Alfred Nzo, Duma Nokwe and Joe Slovo.

But Mwalimu Nyerere was not just a leader; he was a statesman. I have deliberately avoided calling him a politician, because politicians come and go. Statesmen live on - the impact of their presence in society is felt for many years after their death. If I can paraphrase William Shakespeare, the good they do lives after them. I found Mwalimu Nyerere to be most articulate, supremely good at putting complex issues in very simple language and very effective in relating to his audience.

Many definitions have been rendered as to who is an intellectual. Is it somebody who has been to a university or, as Ali Mazrui once put it, "one who is excited by ideas and has acquired the ability to handle some of these ideas effectively"? Is it a professional or one who can stand up and talk on Picasso, Leo Tolstoy or Beethoven?

Byron considered an intellectual not only a person attracted to ideas, but whose purpose in life, whose thought and actions were determined by those ideas. Issa Shivji holds that one of the important attributes of an intellectual is "the ability to laugh at ourselves."

I consider an intellectual as not only a person who is able to analyse the present but is also able to articulate ideas that would have a lasting impact on those who receive them. But whatever definition one might adopt, of importance is the fact that the role of an intellectual in any society is enormous.

Western education in Africa, especially in Southern Africa, is a recent phenomenon. Pre-colonial African societies, with few exceptions, had no formal educational systems. But if the purpose of any education, as Julius Nyerere put it, "is to transmit from one generation to the next the accumulated wisdom and knowledge of the society, and to prepare the young people for their future membership of the society and their active participation in its maintenance and development," then these societies had appropriate educational systems.

The aim of western education, which came with colonialism, was to instil in the minds of its recipients an idolisation for the superiority of the colonial master. First it was the sons of chiefs and other traditional leaders that received this education; and later, with the expansion of the colonial economy, more and more people acquired it. Budo, Kisubi, Fort Hare, Makerere, were all created for that purpose. The aim was to produce clerks, teachers, priests, agricultural extension workers, hospital assistants, and others, to help in the running of the colonial machinery.

University education was restricted to only a few. It was only after independence that education became accessible to more people. Of the few that received western education, not all acted according to the expectations of the colonial regime. Some turned out to be the most vehement opponents of the colonial system not only in the political and economic spheres, but also in the areas of education, culture, and others. The reasons are obvious.

Colonialism affected both the traditional chief and the ordinary worker. It did not even allow the emergence of the native capitalist. While in the colonial possessions of Asia and semi-colonial China, a local compradorial class was allowed to exist, in most of Africa this class did not emerge. It is no wonder then that in most of the African states the harbingers of the nationalist movements were people coming from the colonial bureaucracy.

The countries of Southern Africa are not a homogeneous group. There are differences in history, culture and experiences. Even those that were ruled by the same colonial power, like Zimbabwe and Tanzania, or Angola and Mozambique, have differences in their social compositions and levels of economic development. There are amongst them countries that attained independence peacefully, such as Tanzania and Swaziland, and others, like Mozambique, Angola and Zimbabwe, which attained it through the barrel of a gun.

Due to the specific conditions of the countries of the region, each one traversed the independence path in her own way. And each country brought to the fore of the independence movements a group of individuals who by any definition can be called intellectuals. What was common in almost all the countries is the fact that this group comprised people with the highest commitment to the ideals of independence and dedication to their achievement.

The backgrounds of this highly politically active intelligentsia vary. In the case of Tanzania Mainland whose economy was basically peasant-based and where education in the early colonial days was mostly provided by Christian missionary schools, the products of such a set-up were people whose vision did not go beyond the peasant collective. This was different from a place such as South Africa where a large section of the community had been uprooted from their land, a numerically strong working class had been formed and where an independent political organisation of this class existed. The logical tendency in this kind of situation would be to produce intellectuals who, to quote Amilcar Cabral, would know where the struggle for national independence ends and the struggle for social emancipation begins.

One of the successes of the colonial system in the region was that it was able to produce an academia that was dependent on western intellectual production. This intelligentsia understood what was taking place in other societies, but lacked adequate knowledge of its own societies. This is what prevailed for a very long time in the African universities.

Admittedly, a few Individuals were to be found in the universities who went against the general mould, but the pattern was for the universities to be replicas of their western peers. As Mwalimu Nyerere stated, "Our universities have aimed at understanding Western society, and being understood by Western society, apparently assuming that by this means they were preparing their students to be - and themselves being - of service to African society." The University of Dar es Salaam was the first in the region to break out of this mould.

Started in 1961 as a constituent college of the University of East Africa (itself enjoying a cooperative status with the University of London), the University College of Dar es Salaam became a full university in 1970 when a decision was taken by the three East African states to each form its own national university. The University of Dar es Salaam in its curricula and research agenda tried to break away from the paradigms set up by others. It aimed at inculcating a sense of commitment to society, and tried to make all who came into contact with it accept the new values appropriate to the post-colonial society. There was a deliberate attempt to fight intellectual arrogance because it was felt that such arrogance had no place in a society of equal citizens.

The University of Dar es Salaam also played its part in the intellectual development of the region. In the ten-year period from

1967 to 1977, the university was a major cooking pot of ideas, and provided a splendid platform for debate and discussion. No African scholar, leader or freedom fighter could ignore its environs. While the government brought its official guests to see its picturesque, Mount Olympius-like exterior, others came to seek knowledge or refine their ideological positions.

Here, the East and West Germans, who officially were not talking to each other; the Chinese and the Americans, who officially could not stand each other; and the white and black South Africans, who at home could not even sit together in the same church, met in the seminar rooms built by Swedes and the British to debate not only on Tanzania's development path but also the Vietnam war, the Palestinian Question, apartheid, the Chinese Cultural Revolution and countless other subjects. Very intense were these debates, and a huge number of discourses and manuscripts were churned out.

That kind of atmosphere existed partly due to conditions created by the Arusha Declaration - the country's policy document on Socialism and Self-Reliance - and partly due to the liberal-mindedness of Mwalimu Julius Nyerere who was the university college's Visitor, and after the establishment of the University of Dar es Salaam, its first Chancellor.

But one also must not under-estimate the impact that the presence of the liberation movements had on Tanzania's intellectual development. These movements were not only engaged in struggles in their respective countries, but their leading cadres, as a result of these struggles, were forced to constantly refine their theories and assumptions; and they found the university campus an excellent testing ground for that exercise.

Thus during the course of this process, the liberation movements not only brought in their towering figures, but also their dissidents and the harbingers of future conflicts. From FRELIMO of Mozambique came people like the religio-tribalist Rev Urio Simango, the liberal minded nationalist Dr Eduardo Mondlane, and the Marxist poet Marcelino dos Santos; from the ANC of South Africa, people like Duma Nokwe, Joe Jele and Ambrose Makiwane; PAC brought Lebalo and Gora Ebrahim; and the MPLA of Angola, Agostinho Neto and the future Nito Alves elements. The Communist Party of South Africa brought in its towering giants, Yusuf Daddoo, Moses Madbida and Joe Slovo.

Since I am in Cape Town, I should also mention that the Unity Movement also had its people appearing on the Dar es Salaam campus. Some of the most significant statements of these movements were made at the University Hill, including the famous one by Neto in 1974, before Angola's independence, on 'Who is the Enemy?' that has remained to this day the MPLA's weightiest document.

Sometime the staff houses on campus were turned into seminar rooms or places for social interaction. There were even times when they were used as hideouts when some leaders of liberation movements did not want their presence in the country publicly known. I remember occasions when Yusuf Dadoo and Joe Slovo (and if my memory does not fail me, Thabo Mbeki, the present President of South Africa, too) came to the university to 'reflect'.

The Tanzanian press at the time provided a very useful platform for debate and discussion. *The Nationalist* (the ruling party's paper) was under the editorship of Benjamin Mkapa, the current President of Tanzania; and the government newspaper, the *Standard*, was under the headship of Dr Frene Ginwala (the former Speaker of the South African Parliament}, as Managing Editor and Mwalimu Nyerere was the Editor-in-Chief. Apart from providing the news, these newspapers also published articles of high quality, and opened their pages for serious debates both on internal and international issues.

People from different parts of the world came to teach at Dar es Salaam. They were brought by different reasons. There were some who simply needed an African experience, but in a surrounding appeasing to their consciences; there were others who were moved by the country's revolutionary potential, and being internationalists, felt that they needed to contribute; and still others, taking pauses from their own struggles, needed breathing space and periods of reflection.

It was definitely the most international university one could ever find in the Third World. Some of the people who came were directly from schools themselves and therefore Dar es Salaam constituted their 'baptism'; others were accomplished academics with international renown.

Names of South Africans that easily come to mind are those of

Ruth First, Archie Mafeje, Denis Brutus, Willy Kogkositle (the former husband of the present Speaker of the South African Parliament), Harold Wolpe, Bob Leshoai, Sixghashe, Dan O'Meara and his former wife, Linzi Manicom and Tshabalala (the former husband of the present South Africa Minister for Health).

From within the Eastern and Southern Africa region, there came Nathan Shamuyarira who later on became Foreign Minister of Zimbabwe; Ibbo Mandaza, Miti and Frank Mbengo, all also from Zimbabwe; Orton Chirwa, the first Justice Minister in Malawi, and his wife, Vera (now a member of the African Commission for Human and People's Rights) and Mutharika, the brother of the present Malawian President; Tunguru Huaraka from Namibia; Mahmoud Mamdani (who is known to this university), Yash Tandon and Dan Nabudere from Uganda; and Yash Ghai from Kenya.

But people came also from far flung areas, including Guyanese historian and political activist Walter Rodney; the Hungarian economist Tamas Szentes; the Nigerian political scientists Okwudiba Nnoli and Claude Ake; the Ghanaians Aki Sawyer and Emanuel Hansen; the British historians Terence Ranger and John Illiffe, political scientist Lionel Cliffeand economists John Loxley and Peter Lawrence; the Canadians, Cranford Pratt who in fact was the first Principal of the university college and John Saul; and many others from Denmark, the United States and other shores. When I was in the then German Democratic Republic in 1985 for a conference on African studies, I found out that many of their Africa specialists had been to Dar es Salaam.

Many people, like Boutros Ghali, who was a university professor before he became a Minister in Egypt and later on the first African Secretary-General of the U.N., and Adebayo Adedeji, the former Executive Secretary of the U.N. Economic Commission for Africa, included a stopover at the University Hill in their schedule whenever they happened to be in Dar es Salaam.

Yoweri Museveni, a few months before he marched into Kampala, went to the university campus to see his old friends; and on his first state visit to Tanzania, he went to deliver a public lecture at the university. The Rivonia heroes, after their release from Robben Island prison, passed through Dar es Salaam on their way to Sweden to meet Oliver Tambo, and they came to the university to talk to the community.

Many academics have achieved fame from intellectual works they produced while in Dar es Salaam. Walter Rodney's legendary book, *How Europe Underdeveloped Africa*, that of Clive Thomas, *On Problems of Transition*, and Tamas Szentes' classic, *The Political Economy of Underdevelopment*, were all written in Dar es Salaam.

The university was not only a haven for radical scholars and activists; the students also found it an exciting and productive experience. Issa Shivji, in his student days, had already produced *Tanzania: The Silent Class Struggle*; and the current President of Uganda, Yoweri Museveni, Kapote Mwakasungura who later on became Malawian High Commissioner to Zimbabwe, Salim Msoma, the present Principal Secretary in the Tanzania Ministry of Transport and Communications, and Andrew Shija who after graduation joined the Tanzania Army, left their classrooms and joined FRELIMO cadres in the liberated areas of Portuguese-ruled Mozambique. A Canadian political scientist, John Saul, when teaching at Dar es Salaam University, did the same thing. The students' journal, *Cheche* [*The Spark*], subsequently *Maji Maji*, was very much sought after, and the teaching staff vied with each other to have their articles published in it.

From its inception in 1961 as a university college until 1985 when he stepped down as the Chancellor, Mwalimu Nyerere played an important role in the shaping of the university, and took a keen personal interest in its intellectual development. I do not think there was any national institution that he visited as many times as the university.

Mwalimu Nyerere was born on 13th April 1922 in the small village of Butiama among a minority ethnic group in Tanzania. He grew up in typical African village surroundings, and later on in life became the embodiment of the African struggle for freedom and national independence and a symbol of people's aspirations for social emancipation and human fulfilment.

It was at the age of 12 that he started going to school, and only after coming of age was he confirmed to Christianity. From Tabora School, the citadel of African education at the time in the then Tanganyika, he then proceeded to Makerere College in Uganda to acquire a Diploma in Education. Makerere was at that time the highest institution of learning in East Africa, and constituted an important period for Mwalimu Nyerere in formulating the objectives and principles that guided him later on in his life. After he left Makerere, he stated the following:

> While I was at Makerere I understood that my Government was spending annually something in the neighbourhood of 80 pounds on my behalf. But that did not mean very much to me: after all, 80 pounds is only a minute fraction of the total amount which is collected every year from the African tax-payers. But today that 80 pounds has grown to mean a very great deal to me. It is not only a precious gift but a debt that I can never repay.
>
> I wonder whether it has ever occurred to many of us that while that 80 pounds was being spent on me (or for that matter on any of the past or present students of Makerere) some village dispensary was not being built in my village or some other village. People may actually have died through lack of medicine merely because eighty pounds which could have been spent on a fine village dispensary was spent on me, a mere individual, instead.
>
> Because of my presence at the college, (and I did nothing to deserve Makerere) many Aggreys and Booker Washingtons remained illiterate for lack of a school to which they could go because the money which could have gone towards building a school was spent on Nyerere, a rather foolish and irresponsible student at Makerere.
>
> My presence at the college therefore deprived the community of the services of all those who might have been trained at those schools, and who might have become Aggreys or Booker Washingtons.
>
> How can I repay this debt to the community? …… The community spends all that money upon us because it wants us as lifting levers, and as such we must remain below and bear the whole weight of the masses to be lifted, and we must facilitate that task of lifting.

From Makerere, Mwalimu Nyerere taught briefly before he proceeded to do a Master's degree in History at the University of Edinburgh in Scotland. He was the first Tanganyika African to acquire an overseas degree. It was in Edinburgh that his political ideas were crystallised.

Upon his return to the then Tanganyika he taught for some time in the Christian Mission schools before he threw himself fully into the nationalist struggle for independence. The Tanganyika African Association (TAA), founded in 1929 by traders and civil servants in urban areas, was basically a social organisation. Only in 1954 was it transformed into a political one, and was known as a Tanganyika African National Union; and Nyerere became its President.

As I have stated, Julius Nyerere has dominated the Tanzanian political and intellectual scene for almost five decades, and even now with his death, his influence is still felt. I will try here to briefly look at some of his ideas.

In his *Ujamaa - The Basis of African Socialism*, Mwalimu Nyerere dismissed the idea that classes had existed in pre-colonial African societies, claiming instead that these societies were living in tranquillity and peace and had experienced no antagonistic contradictions. He felt that it was possible for Africans, regardless of their social backgrounds, to come together in national movements and to retain that unity after independence. He not only dismissed the notion of the existence of classes prior to colonisation but did not see their evolution during the colonial period

In 1967 Tanzania declared its intention to build socialism on the basis of self-reliance. Julius Nyerere was definitely the intellectual power behind the Declaration. In fact Jeanette Hartmann has stated that it was written by Nyerere himself, claiming that she had seen the draft in Mwalimu Nyerere's handwriting. The Declaration attracted huge attention.

To social democrats in Europe this heralded the possibility of seeing the realisation of their ideals in an African set-up. Imperialist powers, on the other hand, were afraid that Tanzania would set up an example to the rest of Africa. From 1967, then, Tanzania's actions on the domestic and international arenas were judged in accordance with the terms of the Arusha Declaration.

Its close relationship with China or its acceptance of aid from the then socialist countries of Eastern Europe was seen as tendencies to further integrate Tanzania within the socialist orbit. But, as Julius Nyerere kept reiterating, the Arusha Declaration should have been viewed as a statement of intent. Neither in 1967 nor in 1985 when he stepped down from the Presidency was Tanzania a socialist state.

The Declaration was not without flaws and its implementation had been far from successful. There were reasons for this; but as a blueprint for development, it was something unique in Africa at that time. It was assertive and provided great hopes for millions of Tanzanians. In another paper - "Socialism: The Rational Choice" - Mwalimu argued that for a country like Tanzania, socialism was the only choice, but even if it wanted to build capitalism, that option was closed to it.

What Mwalimu Nyerere succeeded in doing was to put socialism on the national agenda. One cannot therefore agree with Ali Mazrui and many others who say that socialism was a 'heroic failure' in Tanzania. *The Wall Street Journal* declared:

"He fused Tanzania's 120 tribes into a cohesive state, preventing tribal conflicts plaguing so much of Africa ... Above all, he proved that it is possible to forge a nation whereby vicissitudes of ethnic affiliation are banished from social and political life. He created and promoted a powerful lingua franca, Swahili, which united and educated people."

He preached racial and religious tolerance. Following Mwalimu Nyerere's departure from political power, the country collapsed into the arms of the IMF and the World Bank. When he left the per capita income was $280. In 1998, thirteen years after he left, it was $140; and school enrolment plummeted to 63%. Some of the progressive achievements of the Nyerere era are being eroded, but he will definitely be remembered in history as the person who raised the prospect of socialist development in Tanzania.

Tanzania's contribution on the question of Africa's liberation is well known. Almost all the liberation movements in Africa had enjoyed sanctuary in Tanzania. The OAU Liberation Committee had its headquarters in Dar es Salaam from the time the OAU was established in 1963. Julius Nyerere cannot be separated from the Tanzania position.

It should be remembered that as far back as 1960, when Tanganyika was not even independent, Nyerere published a pamphlet called "Barriers to Democracy" in which he castigated the white communities in Kenya, the Rhodesias and South Africa for rejecting the concept of a multiracial society based on African majority rule. Also in 1961, just before Tanganyika's independence, in an article in the London newspaper *The Observer*, Nyerere made it clear to the British Government that the membership of independent Tanganyika in the Commonwealth will depend on South Africa either ending apartheid or withdrawing from the Commonwealth. Apartheid South Africa decided to withdraw from the Commonwealth.

As stated before, there is no single African liberation movement that did not enjoy the support of Tanzania. FRELIMO was founded in Tanzania; the ANC, after its ban in South Africa, opened its first External Mission in Tanzania; and MOLINACO, MPLA, ZANU, ZAPU, PAC and many others had Tanzania's full support. In the U.N. Decolonisation Committee (known as the Committee of 24), where Tanzania's then Permanent Representative to the U.N., Salim Ahmed Salim, held the Chairmanship for several years, and in the Non-Aligned Movement, Tanzania was in the forefront in mobilising support to the liberation struggles.

Tanzania's support to the liberation movements was not only manifested in the political and diplomatic arenas but also in the material and military fields. The Tanzanian population was mobilised many times to give material support to the liberation movements. The Tanzania People's Defence Forces trained thousands of military cadres of those liberation movements which wanted that kind of support.

Tanzania was used as a facility for either storing or transporting different types of goods to the liberation movements. It is a known fact that several villages along the border with Mozambique were bombed by Portuguese planes during FRELIMO's struggle for independence. All this testifies to the country's firm position on the question of African liberation. But again it was Julius Nyerere who was able not only to give an intellectual basis to this position but also to effectively articulate it.

Julius Nyerere was always non-racial in his perspective, and this at times got him into conflict with his colleagues both in the ruling Party and Government. During the days of the struggle for Tanganyika's independence, he rejected the position of the "Africanists" within TANU who put forward the slogan "Africa for Africans", meaning black Africans. In 1958 at the TANU National Conference in Tabora when some leaders strongly opposed TANU's participation in the colonially-proposed tripartite elections, where the voter had to vote for three candidates from the lists of Africans, Asians and Europeans,

Julius Nyerere stood firm in recommending acceptance of the proposals. This led to the "Africanists" marching out of TANU and forming the African National Congress.

It is extremely worrying that this racist monster is reappearing now in Tanzania. Some politicians in their quest for power are using the racist card, as manifested both at last May's Chimwaga Congress of the ruling party, CCM, and in the on-going election campaigns. It is very unfortunate that no stern measures are being taken against this trend, thus giving the impression that the country's leadership is condoning it.

Again, after independence, when a section of the leadership of TANU and that of the trade union movement, the Tanganyika Federation of Labour, were demanding Africanisation of the civil service, Julius Nyerere was talking of Tanganyikanisation, thus giving a non-racial content to the whole idea.

His commitment to African Liberation stemmed not only from these anti-racist convictions but also from his strong belief that it is evil and wrong for a foreign power to colonise another people, and that it is equally wrong for a racial minority to oppress a racial majority. Mwalimu Nyerere had never doubted that whites in Zimbabwe or South Africa had the same rights as their black compatriots.

Julius Nyerere believed in peaceful means in the struggle to achieve certain political ends. He tried very much during the Tanganyika independence struggle to steer the independence movement along peaceful lines. Even at those times when the temperature was high and militants either in TANU or TFL were calling for confrontation, Julius Nyerere continued to call for restraint. When, after being convicted of libel in a colonial court, he was faced with the option of going to prison or paying a fine, he chose the latter, not so much because he did not want to be a political prisoner, but because it was felt that in his absence things might go wrong and violence might erupt.

However, when faced with a situation where all peaceful means were closed, Mwalimu Nyerere never hesitated to advocate the use of violence against an oppressive regime. A few months before Britain handed over power to the Sultan's regime in Zanzibar, he appealed to the British Government, through its Colonial Secretary, to reconsider its intention because he felt that if the situation was not rectified to allow the majority to peacefully take over power, then violence was inevitable. And on this he was right, because four weeks after independence the Sultan's regime was violently overthrown by opposition parties.

Again, when nationalists in Angola, Guinea-Bissau, Mozambique, the then Southern Rhodesia and South Africa were forced to take up arms against colonial and apartheid regimes, Mwalimu Nyerere committed both Tanzanian resources and his own personal prestige in helping the liberation movements to engage in the armed struggle, and found this to be in no contradiction with his non-violence convictions.

Mwalimu Nyerere's last visit to the University of Dar es Salaam was in December 1997 when he came to take part in the international conference on Reflections on Leadership in Africa - Forty Years after Independence. The conference was in honour of his 75th Birthday and was organised jointly by the Institute of Development Studies of the University of Dar es Salaam and the Mwalimu Nyerere Foundation. Nkrumah Hall at the university, with a capacity of 500 to 600 people, was full to overflowing. The organisers had expected not more than 100 people.

Ministers, leaders of political parties, academics, students (even though the University was on Christmas vacation), NGO activists, foreign diplomats, media people - they were all there. It was obvious that the centre of attraction was Mwalimu Nyerere, and that they all came to see him and hear him.

After the keynote address by Tanzania Vice-President, the late Dr Omar Ali Juma, Mwalimu Nyerere was asked to speak. He spoke for more than one and a half hours, entirely extempore. It was one of his best speeches, unfortunately the last one at the university. It was full of humour, but also deeply serious, thought provoking, and providing a sense of direction. The audience loved him. That speech has been produced in full in the book that I edited based on the conference papers called *Reflections on Leadership in Africa - Forty Years After Independence*, and was published in 2000 by VUB University Press in Brussels, Belgium.

In that speech, Mwalimu was making one very important point, that Africa South of the Sahara was on its own. North America, meaning the United States and Canada, had to do something to help Mexico, otherwise the Latin wanderers would simply cross over even if a steel wall were erected. The Slavs, Croatians, Czechs and others in Eastern Europe would be attracted to Western Europe, and the North Africans would be interested in Southern Europe. The South East Asians would be looking to Japan. But Africans South of the Sahara had no 'uncle' to depend on. We were on our own. We have to rely on ourselves, and to cooperate among ourselves.

After the opening ceremony, the conference went into workshops. In the workshops where Mwalimu Nyerere was participating, he was very active, speaking with his usual lucidity of elaboration and illustration. In one session, the audience was pensive, watching him exchanging views with Issa Shivji on the land question; and at another he explained why he had to ask a group of freedom fighters to leave the country, an issue that was raised in the paper presented by a Russian scholar on African affairs, Vladimir Shubin.

After one of the sessions, Mwalimu Nyerere wanted the South African academic, Patrick Bond, and a few others to follow him to his Msasani residence to continue with the discussion. Bond had raised the issue of Afrikaner capital in the Southern Africa region and the way it was behaving.

Mwalimu Nyerere's last intellectual work was the translation into Kiswahili of Plato's *The Republic*. As he was lying in bed at London's St. Thomas Hospital, he went through the manuscript, made the necessary corrections and completed them before he died. Unfortunately the work has not yet been published.

Mwalimu Nyerere was not a saint (though, according to press reports, there are discussions now amongst the Catholics in his native area to request the Church to start the process of beatifying him) and he did commit a number of mistakes. But his patriotism was unmistaken, his commitment and devotion to Africa unquestionable and his integrity outstanding. His achievements were many, and leaders in Tanzania (and in Africa), present and future ones, will be judged according to the yardsticks set by people like Mwalimu Julius Nyerere.

At present the Southern African sub-continent is facing a deep crisis: legacies of colonialism and white domination, underdevelopment, debt problem, HIV/AIDS and natural and unnatural calamities. All these pose serious challenges to the intelligentsia of the region.

The intellectuals of the colonial past could have been lured to the colonial trappings but decided to join the independence movement. The present intelligentsia have nothing to lure them into the post-colonial state. Our role is to transform our societies and to give content to human dignity. One should live so that in dying one can say: I gave all my strength for the liberation of humanity.

References:

Kierman, V. G. (1969). "Notes on the Intelligentsia", *The Socialist Register.*

Lerumo A (1971). "Fifty Fighting Years - The South African Communist Party 1921- 1971," London: Inkululeko Publication.

Mamdani, M. (1986). "Our Political Role Today: Problems and Prospects," *UDASA Newsletter/Forum.*

Mandaza, I. (1988). "The Relationship of Third World Intellectuals and Progressive Western Scholars: An African Critique," SAPES No. 5 February.

Miliband and Panitch (eds). (1990). "The Retreat of Intellectuals," *The Socialist Register.*

Nyerere, J. K. (1966). "The Role of Universities."

------- (1967). "Education for Self-Reliance."

------- (1968). "The Intellectual Needs of Society."

------- (1970). "Relevance and Dar es Salaam University."

Nyong'o, P. A. (1988). "African Intellectuals and the State," SAPES No.5.

Othman, Haroub (1980). "Homage to a Committed Intellectual: Jean Paul Sartre."

------- (1983). "Committed Scholarship and the Search for a Progressive Development Path in Southern Africa," SADRA Congress, Maseru, Lesotho.

------- (1986). The Political Legacy of Julius Nyerere, SOAS, London.

------- (1992). "The Intellectual and Transformation in Southern Africa," University of Western Cape.

------- (2000). *Reflections on Leadership in Africa: Forty Years After Independence*, VUB University Press, Brussels.

Shivji, I. G. (1986). "Intellectuals in Crisis and the Crisis of Intellectuals," *UDASA Newsletter/Forum.*

About the Author

Godfrey Mwakikagile comes from Tanzania. He has written a number of books mostly about Africa. His works include *Africa and the West*; *The Modern African State: Quest for Transformation*, and *Life in Tanganyika in the Fifties: My Reflections and Narratives from the White Settler Community*.

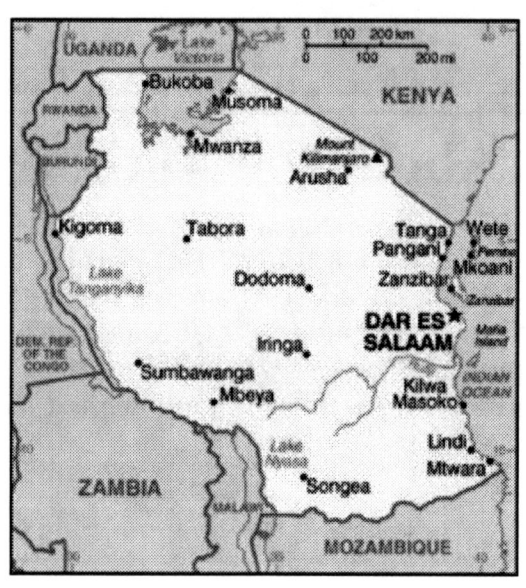

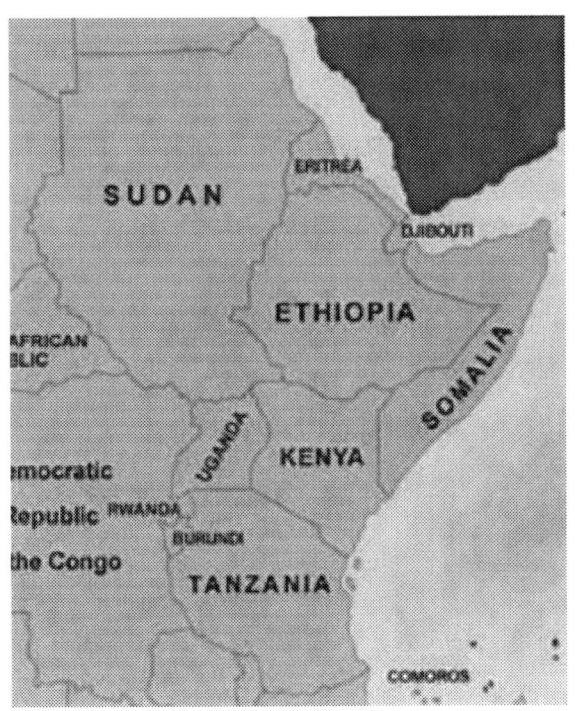

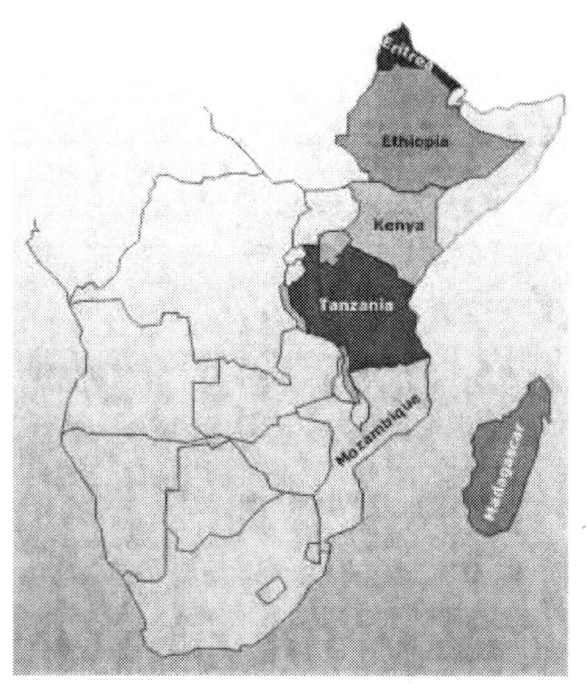

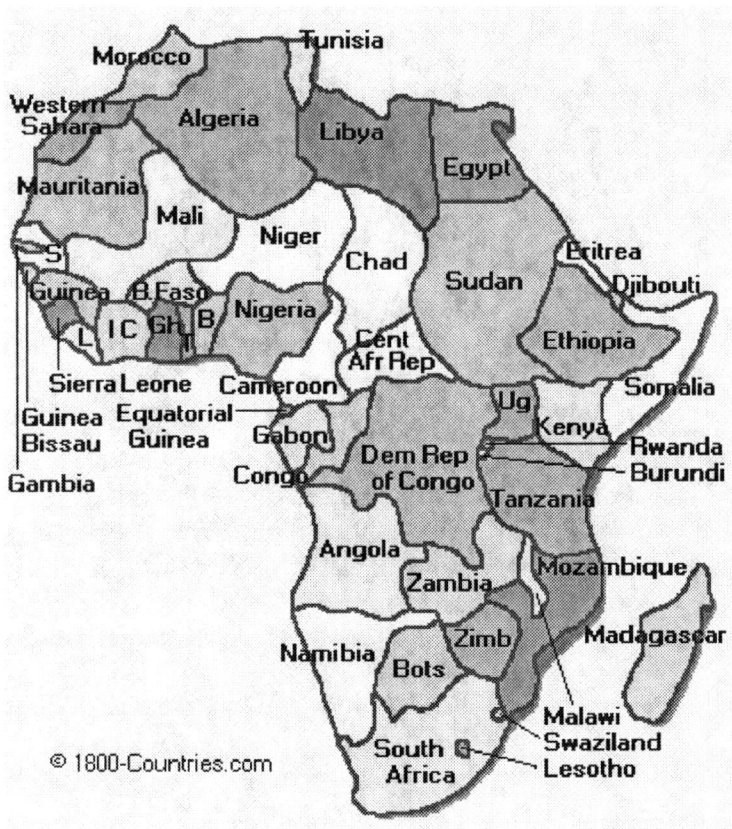